"Perfect for professional learning sessions, this book offers practical examples and experiences to help teachers discuss their questions while reconsidering their beliefs about how children learn."

Geri Cunningham, *Elementary Principal, Kansas City, Kansas*

"*Constructivist Teaching by Heart* feels like a conversation with the authors without using a lot of educational jargon. It brings back developmentally appropriate, child-centered teaching with practical, relatable examples."

Rebecca McGregor, *2nd Grade Teacher, Enumclaw, Washington*

"This book reminds us to see school through the eyes of a child who loves to explore, discover, create, and learn. It will remind you of why you fell in love with learning, and show you how to pass on that love to the learners, leaders and thinkers of our next generation. A delightful, thought-provoking, desperately needed resource as we strive to provide the best education for our children."

Dr. Jennifer Waddell, *Director of Teacher Education, University of Missouri – Kansas City*

"This book is full of practical, high-impact teaching ideas that provide opportunities to teach from the heart. The literature connections lists are pure gold."

Christi Clayton, *Language Instructional Coach, Olathe, Kansas*

"I wish I had this book when I started teaching!"

Judy Fink, *Kindergarten Teacher, Kansas City, Missouri*

Constructivist Teaching by Heart

This insightful book offers a modern take on the time-honored tradition of developmentally appropriate, child-centered, constructivist philosophy of instruction: Teaching children one at a time, yet all at once. The book provides a comprehensive road map to teaching that supports student engagement, child development, classroom environment, grouping and organization, authentic literacy instruction, and culturally informed practices.

Through a series of practical chapter essays and examples, the authors push back against scripted curricula and "one-size-fits-all" school initiatives, offering instead rich examples and guiding questions to bring you closer to an authentic teaching approach that honors students and their learning.

Designed for early childhood through third-grade teachers, principals, administrators, and pre-service students, *Constructivist Teaching by Heart* is essential reading for professional development, peer discussions, university coursework, individual study, and everyone on the journey to making children the heart of their classrooms.

Krista Calvert, EdD, is currently an elementary reading specialist in Kansas City, Kansas. She has taught elementary and middle school, served as a literacy coach and a school improvement coach, and led school and district-wide literacy initiatives. She teaches master's level reading, children's literature, and literacy intervention courses at Avila University.

Dana McMillan is an education consultant working with educators on student engagement centered around a constructivist theory. Dana has dual degrees in elementary and early childhood education and a master's degree in literacy education and taught early primary grades. She has consulted on the development of child-centered experiential learning programs for organizations throughout the United States.

Other Eye on Education Books
Available from Routledge
(www.routledge.com/eyeoneducation)

The Heart-Centered Teacher
Restoring Hope, Joy, and Possibility in Uncertain Times
Regie Routman

Pause, Ponder, and Persist in the Classroom
How Teachers Turn Challenges into Opportunities for Impact
Julie Schmidt Hasson

Teach from Your Best Self
A Teacher's Guide to Thriving in the Classroom
Jay Schroder

Leadership for Safe Schools
The Three Pillar Approach to Supporting Students' Mental
Health
Philip J. Lazarus and Michael L. Sulkowski

Your First Year
How to Survive and Thrive as a New Teacher, Second Edition
Todd Whitaker, Madeline Whitaker Good, and Katherine Whitaker

Supporting Student Mental Health
Essentials for Teachers
Michael Hass and Amy Ardell

Constructivist Teaching by Heart
A Child-Centered Approach for Educators, PreK-3
Krista Calvert and Dana McMillan

Constructivist Teaching by Heart

A Child-Centered Approach for Educators, PreK-3

Krista Calvert and Dana McMillan

Routledge
Taylor & Francis Group

NEW YORK AND LONDON

Designed cover image: © Getty Images

First published 2024
by Routledge
605 Third Avenue, New York, NY 10158

and by Routledge
4 Park Square, Milton Park, Abingdon, Oxon, OX14 4RN

Routledge is an imprint of the Taylor & Francis Group, an informa business

© 2024 Taylor & Francis

Library of Congress Cataloging-in-Publication Data
Names: Calvert, Krista, author. | McMillan, Dana, author.
Title: Constructivist teaching by heart : a child-centered approach for educators, PreK-3 / Krista Calvert and Dana McMillan.
Description: New York, NY : Routledge, 2024. | Series: Eye on education | Includes bibliographical references.
Identifiers: LCCN 2023054741 | ISBN 9781032707914 (hardback) | ISBN 9781032686752 (paperback) | ISBN 9781032707921 (ebook)
Subjects: LCSH: Early childhood education--Curricula. | Education, Elementary--Curricula. | Constructivism (Education) | Student-centered learning. | Child development.
Classification: LCC LB1139.4 .C35 2024 | DDC 372.21--dc23/eng/20231227
LC record available at https://lccn.loc.gov/2023054741

ISBN: 978-1-032-70791-4 (hbk)
ISBN: 978-1-032-68675-2 (pbk)
ISBN: 978-1-032-70792-1 (ebk)

DOI: 10.4324/9781032707921

Typeset in Palatino
by SPi Technologies India Pvt Ltd (Straive)

We dedicate this book to our parents. Krista's dad was a beloved high school coach and physical education teacher who strived to share the joy of lifelong sports. He was known for being fair and caring, often championing students given up on by others. Dana's mother went back to college after raising her own family to become a high school art teacher who loved to instill an appreciation for the arts in her students. Two small-town girls (Iowa and Missouri) with a passion for education developed in them from a young age who found each other in a big city and discovered their shared enthusiasm for child-centered teaching.

Contents

Conclusion: From Our Teachers' Hearts to Yours. 163

Introduction

Are You a Constructivist Teacher?

We know many teachers are out there withering on the vine of checklists, mandates, and passive learning requirements. You came into this profession because you love to work with children, observe how they learn, and see the "ahas" and lightbulbs go on! You use these observations to direct where you go next with each child. We see you. We believe you can still be a constructivist teacher.

What Is *Constructivist Teaching by Heart*?

Highly effective teachers work with students individually while creating a community of learners. Constructivism means putting the child at the center of their learning so they can actively construct meaning and add this to their knowledge base. Constructivist teachers meet children where they are, planning experiential lessons that build on what is already known by the child. Using evidence-based teaching practices, teaching by heart means being present and attentive to students and

DOI: 10.4324/9781032707921-1

the classroom community. You adapt the curriculum in the best interest of your students to stay true to your beliefs. You are open to changing methods when you learn of a better way.

Constructivist teachers are thoughtful about each aspect of the learning day and schedule it to maximize learning. As life-long learners, constructivist teachers rely on regular, in-depth discussions about this work we love. Supporting those conversations is the purpose of this book.

How to Use This Book

Constructivist Teaching by Heart is designed to be used by educators serving preK–3rd-grade students as they work in professional development sessions- possibly in grade-level teams, professional learning communities, individually, or as an entire staff. Chapters are organized into broad topics. Each chapter is composed of essays designed to explore the topic. At the end of each essay is an example from our own experiences and a set of questions to consider. We encourage you to have a book study or keep a notebook of your thinking and discuss the questions with your colleagues. We hope you create more questions to continue the discussions as far as they take you.

Children's books are a large part of a constructivist teacher's toolbox. Therefore, recommended children's literature is often included within each chapter. We like to use children's books in our professional development sessions, and you may also find the literature suggestions work well in your curriculum.

In reading this book, you are encouraged to

♦ read the essay,
♦ consider the real-life examples and children's literature offered, and
♦ explore the discussion questions and think of questions of your own.

It is not necessary to follow the book in any particular order. Choose the chapters that work best for your situation and move at your own pace in the most useful order.

Am I a Constructivist, a Behaviorist...or Somewhere In Between?

Constructivist teaching is grounded in the belief that students learn and grow through carefully constructed lessons, learning themes, and open-ended activities offering a range of potential learning outcomes. Through these experiences, each student adds to their base of knowledge. Through a teacher's understanding of what children know and how this learning can be built, students create knowledge, put it in context, and express it in their language.

Children integrate new learning into what is known by constructing their ideas, incorporating them into their vocabulary, and then expressing them verbally, on paper, or through actions. Behaviorist activities such as filling in the blank, completing the worksheet, or mastering practice tests are the opposite. They offer little opportunity to construct knowledge.

Now, we are not saying behaviorism is a bad thing. Sometimes, we must fill in the blanks or complete the sentence stem. For example, driver's education. We all need the same information as the traffic rules are applied. It is fine to fill in the blanks on the driver's exam. We need every driver to memorize the facts precisely the same, right? I (Dana) have always said I likely want a behaviorist surgeon. Follow the procedure strictly, and ensure each step is done correctly.

However, do we need every reader to memorize a set of identical words in the same order – or even letters? No, readers will learn the same words but not in the same order, even when the teacher only teaches one word at a time or one letter at a time. Children will learn the words incorporated into their language (words meaningful for them) and the letters that have meaning to them first, such as the letters in their names.

In my (Krista) daughter Olivia's case, she first learned O for apparent reasons. When she was around three, she saw Os everywhere. I remember one week when we took her older brother to zoo camp, and we would pass the Kansas City Zoo sign every day. Olivia would yell – "O-O-Z – Zoo!" I think she saw the Os first because they belonged to her.

Later on, when Olivia started kindergarten, she knew all the letters in her first and last name but had yet to firm up the rest of the alphabet. Interestingly, Olivia's best friend in kindergarten was Kimberly Gunderson. She learned how to write Kimberly's name right away, and between the two names, Olivia Smith had only a few letters left to learn. I still do not know how her wonderful kindergarten teacher taught the alphabet (all at once or one letter at a time) because it didn't matter.

Are you a constructivist? Here is a short list of possible identifiers of constructivist teachers using American comedian Jeff Foxworthy's "You might be a redneck if" analogy.

You know you might be a constructivist if…

- ♦ Your bulletin boards are full of students' work.
- ♦ Your students are sometimes doing different things at different times.
- ♦ You consider conversation a learning tool used throughout the school day.
- ♦ You adapt curricular materials when needed.
- ♦ You teach children where they are and build from there.
- ♦ You honor the background and ethnicity of each child.
- ♦ You reach for growth, not perfection.
- ♦ Your students enjoy school.
- ♦ You rarely need to employ sticker charts or extrinsic rewards for learning.
- ♦ You celebrate students' learning and growth often.
- ♦ Your students talk as much as you do during the school day.
- ♦ You let the students get to know you, and you get to know them.
- ♦ You compare each student to themselves.
- ♦ Your bulletin boards have few cookie-cutter images.
- ♦ You use authentic materials as much as possible.
- ♦ You use your normal voice.
- ♦ You reject "one-size-fits-all" teaching.
- ♦ You have high expectations for each child.
- ♦ Your classroom contains trade books, individual book boxes, manipulatives, and activity centers.

◆ When the principal walks in, they see a busy beehive of activity but may be unable to identify one objective (because many objectives are being met simultaneously).

If these are examples of teaching that you value, then you might be a constructivist teacher.

Let's compare our observations of constructivists and behaviorists in education:

Constructivist – MORE putting your own language on the page

Behaviorist – MORE filling in the blank, completing the workbook

Constructivist – MORE creating with tablets, blocks, and stories

Behaviorist – MORE filling in an already determined pattern

Constructivist – MORE using technology to complete a project

Behaviorist – MORE using technology for skill-and-drill or test prep activities

Constructivist – MORE natural consequences

Behaviorist – MORE predetermined consequences

Constructivist – MORE allowing students to make mistakes and learn from those mistakes

Behaviorists – MORE taking away choices to keep students from making mistakes

Constructivist – MORE making adaptations because one size never fits all

Behaviorists – MORE one-size-fits-all lesson planning and instruction

Constructivist – MORE small-group and individualized learning activities

Behaviorist – MORE students doing the same thing as the whole group across the school day

Constructivist – MORE performance, portfolio, anecdotal, and self-assessment, along with regular state and local measures

Behaviorist – MORE predictive, diagnostic, interim, standardized assessment, along with regular state and local measures

Constructivist – MORE on-task talking, turn and talk, and conversational language used all day

Behaviorist – MORE students sitting in their seats quietly, raising their hands to speak

Think back to your childhood teachers. Constructivists or behaviorists? You can probably divide them into two general groups. We will go into constructivism and behaviorism more deeply in Chapter 1, looking first at descriptors and characteristics, and then at dispositions for learning, caring for children, and engagement in learning. Finally, we will come back to how each author's constructivist journey began.

1

What Is Teaching by Heart?

Constructivist and Behaviorist: Piaget vs. Skinner (Dana)

My coauthor, Krista Calvert, and I are constructivists, but we have come to understand that we live in a behaviorist world. In education, these two distinctive philosophies are often in conflict. As a result, we have experienced many successes as well as frustrations. Creating our classrooms, teaching and working with colleagues, and discussing our philosophy with educators and families are at the heart of our constructivist journey. Through the years, we continue to learn and grow through our many conversations and experiences.

So, what is a constructivist? The term "constructivist" comes from the work of Jean Piaget, a Swiss-born psychologist who advocated that children "construct" meaning from their experiences. This theory was based on his research on the psychological development of children. Thus, the term constructivism.

In contrast, behaviorism comes primarily from the work of American B. F. Skinner. He proposed that learning should be presented in small, sequential steps designed by adults. He believed that children come to school as "empty vessels," and the adult's role in education is to fill the vessel through conditioning, often using rewards to keep students moving along in their learning. A behaviorist classroom environment is fully teacher-led.

Constructivists believe children learn whole-to-part, where their interests in the larger ideas drive the process. This learning

DOI: 10.4324/9781032707921-2

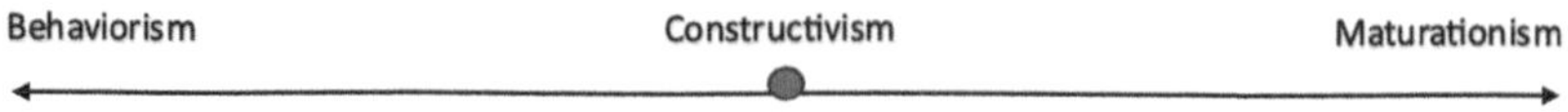

Behaviorism   Constructivism   Maturationism

FIGURE 1.1 Continuum of Learning Theories

process is active and self-directed. Students feel empowered to make decisions about their learning without needing an adult to reward them for their progress. At the turn of the century in the United States, John Dewey based his work on Piaget's research. Dewey believed education should be centered on the learner, children develop in their own time, and learning is social, interactive, and inquiry-based.

Behaviorists and constructivists are far apart. To demonstrate the difference in professional learning sessions, I draw a long line on the board to display the contrast to educators. Like the continuum in Figure 1.1, I place behaviorism on one end of the continuum and the opposite theory, maturationism, on the other end. Seldom seen in the United States, maturationism originated from the work of Arnold Gessell and was advanced by Maria Montessori. Maturationists are the "play" people who believe teachers are to take a passive role in the child's learning process.

In the middle of the two theories is constructivism. Some curricula and curricular materials land more closely to behaviorism, others closer to constructivism. This is the push and pull that Krista and I feel every day in our work.

Many additional learning theories can be placed on this continuum. In fact, we all can place ourselves somewhere on this line based on our beliefs about how children learn. Where are you on the continuum? Is it where you want to be? If we want to make our work with students more about the authentic construction of learning and less about learning one skill or "part" of the whole at a time, we will want to move toward constructivist teaching on this continuum. How do we do that? The answer to that question is the backbone of this book.

Example for Constructivist and Behaviorist: Piaget vs. Skinner

A few years ago, I was preparing Thanksgiving dinner for our family. To get our 11-year-old granddaughter to put down her cell phone and engage more in the event, I said, "Ella, I have the *perfect* job for you." Yes, I was exaggerating, but sometimes, with pre-teens, I find myself resorting to that approach. "What is it?" she asked.

She would say this is my typical "teacher" response. I asked, "How would you like to peel potatoes?" But her answer amazed me. She said, "Well, I've never done it before, but I guess I will figure it out." It warmed my heart! That is a constructivist answer. Constructivists love to figure out something new. They may watch a video on YouTube to see how others peel potatoes, but in the end, they will want to try it for themselves, work out their approach, learn how the potatoes feel, and even figure out what to do with the leftovers.

When I shared this story with Krista, we had fun asking, "What kind of potato peeler are you?" How would other people we know respond, and what does their approach tell us about them as learners? Constructivists come in many sizes, shapes, and approaches. Everyone we could think of would want to figure out potato peeling independently.

We think Krista's son, Russell, an analytical 15-year-old, would say, "Yes, I'll peel potatoes, but only if you have the most innovative, state-of-the-art potato peeler for me to use." Jake, Ella's 16-year-old brother, would watch videos on peeling potatoes and then time himself to see which method is the quickest.

Krista would need to listen to a podcast or something to make it more interesting because she feels like she's been peeling potatoes all her life. And Olivia, Krista's "song and dance" daughter, would turn it into a musical production as she had recently done while raking leaves.

What kind of potato peeler are you? How about the people in your lives? What does it tell us about how we individually construct knowledge?

Questions for Constructivist and Behaviorist: Piaget vs. Skinner:

◆ What kind of potato peeler are you? Think of other activities that would show how we are individual in how we construct knowledge or accomplish authentic tasks.

- ◆ Where do you put your philosophy of education on the continuum? How does that compare with colleagues?
- ◆ What did you already know about these theories of how children learn? What are your beliefs?

REFLECTION BOX A

What questions do you have for

BEHAVIORIST AND CONSTRUCTIVIST: PIAGET VS. SKINNER?

Dispositions (Dana)

Do kids love school? We often answer "no" without hesitation or concern. We have come to accept that children and adults feel it is okay not to like school. Grandparents may laugh when a child answers "no" to their question about how they like school. To enjoy learning is the most basic purpose of schooling. We should not accept that many children do not like school. We can help students create a love of school and learning.

So, how do constructivists approach helping children love school and learning? I believe it is *dispositions*. This is the easiest tool educators have in their toolbox. It is simple. Dispositions are always available, and they change lives. It most certainly changes how children approach school and learning.

According to Lillian Katz (1985), an early childhood educator from the University of Illinois, a disposition is a *habit of the mind*. You gain dispositions by seeing them displayed in someone (often older than you) that you admire. For example, when a parent or a teacher reads an excellent book aloud to a child and makes every character come to life. They read the story with joy and laughter and take time to admire the illustrations in the book. Teachers can wonder aloud about what may be coming up next in the story. These actions create a disposition to love books. The child will wish to read a book just the same way.

You've seen children go to the library area of the classroom, pick up a book recently read to them, and pretend to read it to another child or a stuffed animal. They have discovered a disposition that will last for a lifetime. They will work hard to become a reader because they love it. No one can take that disposition away.

You don't have to know the content to have a disposition for it. I can watch a car race with my husband simply because he loves to watch, shares interesting information, and encourages my questions about racing.

You can have many dispositions. Think about something you love, a hobby, or an activity you love. Is it cooking or baking? Do you love baseball? Are you a history nut? Are you a person who loves to work on cars, read car magazines, or go to car races like my husband? Those are dispositions, and you likely can trace where you gained that disposition. Did you see it in one of your parents, a beloved aunt, or a favorite older brother? Or did you see it in a teacher?

We can pass along dispositions to students in every curriculum area. When preparing to teach a new math concept, we can say, "I am so excited for you to try this new math problem. You'll love how this kind of problem makes you think." Yes, they may have to work hard to figure it out, but if you model that problem-solving is gratifying, you're creating another critical disposition.

New teachers can thrive with experienced teachers who model a caring and thoughtful disposition. We all have had mentors who impacted our teaching practice. They influenced who we would become as teachers.

We often hear about someone from a challenging home situation who went on to higher learning and a successful career. When asked to tell the story of their success, they will often describe someone who came into their life at a young age, demonstrated a belief in their abilities, and gave them a love for learning that changed their lives. Sometimes, that person was an educator, a teacher, or a principal who changed the trajectory of their lives and helped them out of a cycle of crisis and despair. They were given an opportunity to learn productive dispositions.

We must display those dispositions to students and be the people they admire and wish to emulate. It really is that simple.

BOX B   Literature Connections for the Classroom

Check out these brilliant texts – each depicting a child gaining a disposition!

Brick by Brick
by Heidi Woodward Sheffield
Papi is a bricklayer who works hard every day, building brick by brick. His son, Luis, works hard in school and practices climbing, molding, and building just like Papi.

Long Shot: Never Too Small to Dream Big
by Chris Paul and Frank Morrison
Everyone told Chris he was too small to play basketball, yet a few important family members encouraged and supported Chris' big dream and love of the game.

Pecan Pie Baby
by Jacqueline Woodson and Sophie Blackall
Gia's mom is expecting and, with the help of pecan pie, helps Gia come to terms with adding a new member to the family.

Rosie Revere, Engineer
by Andrea Beaty and David Roberts
Rosie Revere loves to invent and build things, but they don't always work. Rosie's great-great-aunt Rose encourages Rosie and helps her understand how to achieve her dream of being an engineer.

Great for a professional development session, this book can help teachers get a glimpse into a constructivist classroom and how the students are affected when a behaviorist practice like high-stakes testing interferes.

First Grade Takes a Test
by Miriam Cohen
When first graders take a standardized test, it becomes clear that there are more important types of learning to experience and celebrate.

Example for Dispositions

Years ago, I had an opportunity to work in a school in England. It was a way for me to see how a British school with a more constructivist theory works. While there, I used trains as my mode of transportation. One Saturday, the train made a stop, and a group of teenagers got into the car where I was riding. They were boisterous and loud. They took some time to settle into their seats, and I admit I was worried they would be disruptive for the trip. But after a few minutes, they quieted down, and to my surprise, they each took a book from their backpacks and quietly began to read.

I was so struck by the fact that each of these teenagers had a book, mostly well-used paperbacks, and they had them ready for the trip they were taking. It caused me to think about American teens. Would they have a book? Would they read on their own when no one expects them to read? It depends on their disposition. I realized this is the hallmark of a disposition: Doing an activity when no one is asking you – such as reading on your own to pass the time on a train trip.

I often use a YouTube video, *Caine's Arcade*, in professional development sessions on this topic. It is the story of a 9-year-old boy in South Los Angeles who loves arcade games. He spends a lot of time with his dad at his used car parts store and has access to cardboard boxes. So, he created his own arcade games out of boxes. He works out detailed processes for how the games will be played, the cost of the games, and even invents a reward system for players who play more often. Unfortunately, no one comes to the arcade he set up in his dad's business. But he continues to build new and progressively more elaborate games. After the video, I ask the participants this question:

Why would a boy work this hard when no one is asking him to?

The discussions are often lively and sometimes emotional because the video pulls at your heartstrings. Still, it makes for an excellent way to discuss dispositions, loving learning, and how we develop dispositions.

Questions for Dispositions:

♦ What do you love to do, and where did you gain the disposition to love this activity?

♦ Where did you get the disposition to be the teacher or educator you are today?

♦ What if you don't like to teach a subject or concept? How can you still make it interesting to your students?

♦ What other dispositions can we demonstrate to our students beyond typical "school subjects"?

REFLECTION BOX C

What questions do you have for

DISPOSITIONS?

Common *Care* Standards (Dana)

There's a much-loved quote by Teddy Roosevelt that can be applied to children's learning: *"No one cares how much you know until they know how much you care."* I believe it's true that children have a harder time learning if they don't think that we care about them. This relates to an interesting twist on standards-based learning. The following quote is from a blog article by Diane Ravitch, who was assistant secretary of education for George H. W. Bush and Bill Clinton. Dianne Ravitch received a response to a comment she had posted online. The writer made a typo; instead of writing *Common Core Standards*, they wrote *Common **Care** Standards*. This text could foster an excellent discussion with your colleagues. Ravitch wrote,

> Wouldn't it be wonderful if our schools had "Common Care Standards," in which we acknowledged our responsibility to care about students? The standards might read like this:

- All children shall have access to high-quality preschool.
- All children should have time to play every day, between classes and after school.
- All children should have three nutritious meals every day.
- All children should see a school nurse whenever they don't feel well.
- All children should be checked by a doctor and dentist annually.
- All children should have access to a well-stocked library.
- All children should have a safe place to live.
- All children should have the arts as part of their daily schedule.
- All children should have a school curriculum that includes not only reading and mathematics, but civics and history, science, literature, and foreign language.

Here are some Common Care Standards Dana would add:

- All children should have highly trained and effective teachers.
- All children should have access to interesting, open-ended materials they can use daily in small groups.
- All children should have the opportunity each day to construct their own meaning on topics they find interesting.

Here are some Common Care Standards Krista would add:

- All children should be treated with dignity and respect.
- All children should see themselves and their world in the classroom literature and environment.
- All children should be given the bandwidth to make mistakes – how will they learn if not?

Finally, we would add one more common care standard – speak kindly, in your normal voice, to other people's children. Teachers often refer to the group of children assigned to their classroom as "my children." But lest we forget, the children's families have entrusted their children to our care, and while in our care, we should teach, protect, guide, and speak to them with kindness.

Of course, there will be times when the teacher is unhappy with student behavior. With a calm teacher in this situation, the students learn how to be unhappy about an event without yelling. Teachers can model how to handle a situation with appropriate consequences, recover from being angry, and resume a positive tone. Children need to know when they have done something unacceptable, but they need to see it as the teacher's disappointment, not a loss of faith. In classrooms where children are spoken to positively, children learn calm and thoughtful ways to interact. They are learning a disposition to be kind in their interactions.

Example for Common Care Standards

I enjoy college basketball, and recently, I saw a game that made me think about how we speak to children. One coach appeared angry from the beginning of the game. He yelled at his players, the referees, and the assistant coaches. He got very close to his players with a very mean look on his face. He was always yelling. He was always mad. He looked so angry. Does this help, I wondered? Did his players need to know how mad he was? Is he always this mad? Interestingly, as the game progressed, I noticed that the players of the "angry coach" were also angry. They began to yell at the referees, too, and soon were yelling at each other. No one looked happy. It's a game, I said to myself. Where is the joy?

I've seen the same thing in schools. Walk down the hallways of a school and listen to how the teachers speak to their students. When you hear a teacher yelling at students, see the angry looks and the hurtful words, do you ask the same question I did? Where is the joy? Often, outside during recess, you can identify the students of the "angry teacher" by how their classroom culture reflects how they speak to each other. Like the basketball team, they often yell at each other, use hurtful words, and say mean things to other children. You see it in the cafeteria, the hallways, moving up and down stairways, and outside waiting to go home. Some classrooms of students are mad all day long.

It doesn't have to be that way. Opposite the "angry coach" during the game I watched was a totally different type of coach. He was intensely engaged in every play as he ran up and down the sidelines, but he appeared to speak calmly in the huddle during time-outs. He allowed his assistant coaches to speak, and it appeared he even encouraged his players to add information to the discussion in a calm tone. During the play, his players encouraged each other. They handed the ball to the referee respectfully. They laughed, and they looked like they were having fun.

The constructivist teacher uses mistakes as a learning tool. Stay calm, speak in a positive tone, and never forget the joy!

Questions for Common Care Standards:

♦ What do you notice about how adults speak to children in your school and classroom?
♦ How can we teach children to interact with others with our tone, body language, and presence?
♦ What common care standards would you include?

REFLECTION BOX D

What questions do you have for

COMMON CARE STANDARDS?

Engagement Is the Heart of Teaching (Dana)

When you read a classic book like *Madeline*, you can see and hear what engagement looks like. When I read *Madeline* to children, I usually take my *Madeline* doll to show children the scar on her abdomen to help them understand why she was in the hospital. What is happening when children are engaged, such as listening to a captivating story?

The story begins:

In an old house in Paris that was covered with vines lived twelve little girls in two straight lines.

At that point, I may ask, "Does anyone know where Paris is?" Some may, and many may not. Here is where the brain gets involved. If they have not heard of Paris or France, they may not have a place in their brains to store any new information from this book. And they won't be able to find the information again when needed. They need to start a file folder. I think of the brain as a file cabinet – with labels and categories – sometimes somewhat unorganized or poorly labeled, possibly needing more information and reorganization. The children do not yet have a file folder if they have not heard of Paris. They can't think about Paris, which makes it hard to be engaged.

So, I may say, "Paris is a big city with this beautiful tower called the Eiffel Tower." I'll show them the book's cover with a picture of the Eiffel Tower. Now, I've started a file folder in their brains. I won't try to fill the file folder with much information at this point – no need to tell them the population or even where it is located. It's just a simple visual to get the file folder started. Later, when I reread the book, which is why I read high-quality books multiple times, I may begin by asking, "Who remembers the city where Madeline lives?" From their answers, I will know if they made a file folder (schema) and, most importantly, if they can retrieve it to begin the engagement.

Young children are creating file folders in their brains with all of their experiences. They label things and file the information into their file folders' categories. With well-labeled items and categories, they can have engagement. However, if a child can't find the information they need, they won't be able to think about it.

For example, very young children may have a file folder in their brains for animals, but it is often mislabeled with the animal they know best. They may call all animals "doggy" because they have had an experience with a dog. Every animal gets placed into a file folder called "doggy." They call cats "doggy." They call squirrels "doggy." All animals are labeled "doggy." The process of organizing and reorganizing their "doggy" file folder takes time, and it depends on an adult helping them put new and correct labels onto each animal they encounter. The child eventually reorganizes their doggy file into separate animals – eventually into animal categories like animals in the zoo, big cats, or pets. When they see a cat and call it "doggy," someone needs to say to them, "That's a cat." When they get a chance to pet a cat, we need to tell them, "That is a cat," even though they may still be thinking dog. It takes time and multiple opportunities to get the cat out of the "doggy" file and into a new, better-organized file. Reading books, seeing a cat, and, most importantly, having a direct experience with a cat makes the case for why young children need as many of these experiences as possible. Without a well-organized file cabinet (brain), children will not pull that file folder, add information to it, and be able to retrieve it to reach full engagement.

So, let's go back to *Madeline*. I may bring a globe to locate Paris to add to the children's "Paris" file folder and help with their engagement. Maybe I will find some pictures of other old houses covered with vines. We can take a walk to look for houses with vines. They may discover that Paris has a zoo, that it rains and snows in Paris, or that a river with a bridge exists. I can add my *Madeline* doll to a learning center, such as the book or dramatic play center. I can put pictures of iconic buildings in the construction center. We can try walking in the hallways in two straight lines. I know the children are becoming more engaged when they ask to reread *Madeline* or initiate a play scenario with *Madeline* as their focus. All the while, their file folder fills with new information, and engagement grows with each step.

Example for Engagement Is the Heart of Teaching

In my kindergarten classroom, I had a well-stocked block center that included a classroom set of unit blocks, miniature people, a set of transportation toys, and other types of blocks, all displayed on open shelves for easy access. The children loved the block center.

One Monday morning, a girl, Gina, who never chose the block center for her center work time, asked to go to the block center, and she announced she would be building an airport. I learned that Gina had driven with her family just the day before to the airport to pick up her grandmother, who was visiting from out of state. This trip made quite an impression on Gina, and she worked the entire time on getting all the airport's details into her construction. For the entire week, Gina built airports. Every day, she added new details, including ticketing desks, baggage areas, and gate waiting rooms. Gina was filling a file folder in her brain with everything she had discovered about airports.

Some other children picked up on Gina's enthusiasm about airports and asked to join her, but she was clearly the lead on any airport work. When Gina and her family returned to the airport for her grandmother's return trip, I asked her parents if they could take pictures for our classroom to see. Those pictures were printed and placed in a prominent spot in the block center, becoming a favorite for all of us.

One child's trip to the airport and an opportunity to show what she had learned by building block structures became a lesson for me on student engagement. Gina knew very little about airports until picking up her grandmother made it worthy of a new file folder in her brain.

Questions for Engagement Is the Heart of Teaching:

♦ When have you seen students become very engaged with a topic or idea? What caused them to want more and more information and experiences?
♦ How could you add to a child's file folder to help them with engagement?
♦ What do we say to educators who want to talk more about covering curriculum and less about engagement?

REFLECTION BOX E

What questions do you have for

ENGAGEMENT IS THE HEART OF TEACHING?

The Heart of a Constructivist

The heart of a constructivist rests on nurturing dispositions for learning, showing children we care, and understanding engagement. So why do we often feel like constructivists in a behaviorist world? The struggle between the two theories of behaviorism and constructivism for Americans is rooted in the fact that most American schools are designed and run with a behaviorist theory framework. It is how we were schooled. It's what we know.

I attended school in my small town. The elementary school was one of the largest and most dominant buildings. The large three-story brick building just off the town square was imposing to small children. It was an old building. Both my parents and grandparents attended this school. I don't know who designed the building, but it was clearly built to carry out behaviorist traditions.

My elementary school was run with many strict rules. You entered the building through the front doors at the top of a walkway. Once inside, you entered a large foyer of green marble. In the middle of the foyer was a school seal. One of the school's many rules was that you were never to walk on the school seal. You must circle to the right and go directly into your classroom. No child was to be caught circling around the foyer. There was a second set of doors directly opposite the front doors. Children who walked to school came in through the front doors, and children who rode to school on buses or cars came in through the back doors. But the same rule applied. Circle to the right, stay off the school seal, and do not pass by your classroom.

My siblings and I walked to school most days and entered the school through the front doors. On rainy or snowy days, my mother drove us and dropped us off in the back of the building. I dreaded inclement weather, even though it was a treat to be driven to school. Why? I feared entering the building from the opposite direction than usual, and in circling from a new direction, I would miss my classroom and be reprimanded for circling around the foyer.

Many years later, after I became a teacher, I reflected on this fear and wondered why a child would be afraid of not locating their classroom. Wouldn't I recognize my classroom? I realized that was the answer. I feared not locating my classroom because they all looked the same. Built by behaviorists, the classrooms were designed with rows of desks bolted onto frames attached to the floor. The teacher's area was placed on a small platform in the front and center of the room. Slightly elevated, it was clear who was in charge.

This design became known as the factory model of education. Invented in the 1860s, its purpose was to standardize the American experience from the top down, develop compliant, well-behaved children, and prepare students for factory work. In this model, you place each child/worker into a small workspace and give them small pieces of work to complete for the person in charge.

Even though we are far removed from preparing students for work in factories, versions of this model continue today. Walk around your school today. Do you see rows of desks? Teachers teaching from their desks? Unless you were lucky enough to attend a "progressive" John Dewey–designed school, the effects of behaviorist schools can make it difficult to envision what a constructivist education can be. We write this book to help navigate the journey from our behaviorist roots to a more constructivist approach for our students.

Where Did Your Constructivist Journey Begin?

I know where my constructivist journey began – in the third grade of that old elementary school I attended. That year, our teacher had a practice clearly rooted in behaviorist theory. Each Monday, she had us all remove everything from our desks and stand around the perimeter of the room while she took out her notebook with the calculations of our scores from the previous week. Then, beginning with seat one in row one, our teacher would point to which of us had the scores necessary to have the privilege of that seat. She continued pointing to the seats and calling out the name of the child who would occupy that desk for the next week. Her tone changed as she moved past the most celebrated seats in row one to show her displeasure at those of us mired somewhere in the middle rows and even more so as she moved to the last couple of rows.

My best friend often claimed seat one or two. If she missed it, she was deeply disturbed for the rest of the week and stressed about achieving the scores she would need to reclaim her prized seat. I don't remember caring much about which chair I would be assigned. I knew it would be somewhere in the middle, and exactly which seat didn't matter to me. But as we stood around the room's edges holding all our belongings, I remember looking at the faces of my friends who were likely to be in those last few rows and thinking to myself, "There must be a better way to do this."

A constructivist was born on those Monday mornings. It was the beginning of my search for another way to do school. I began to play school with my friends, younger siblings, and cousins, not recreating the school I was enduring but dreaming up something new and different. I believe this is where my constructivist journey began.

Krista's constructivist journey also started in elementary school. Krista was one of those quiet kids who always had a book with her. She was an avid reader but got Cs at best in reading class. In fifth grade, all she could remember about the reading curriculum was SRA cards, where you had to read the passage and answer the questions. She hated reading those passages and answering multiple questions about the boring topics. So, she either didn't finish them or often hurried through so she could get to read her book. At the time, Krista often wondered why they couldn't just read books for her reading grades. She thinks that's where her constructivist roots began.

How about you? Where did your journey begin? Maybe yours was in college when you had a particularly compelling professor who presented another way. Or when you student taught with a constructivist teacher? There are so many ways in education we can have new experiences that change our beliefs. What was one thing that helped you think there must be a better way? We hope you write your story and share it.

2

Begin with Child Development

Constructivist teachers consider child development and recognize that each child's development is unique. Every child is on their own journey in all areas of development: cognitive, social, emotional, and language. Therefore, comparing one child to another offers no useful information for instruction. In Chapter 2, we review Piaget's developmental stages, consider social and emotional development, and look at failure and the teacher's role. We will examine if our language about students reflects our beliefs.

Let's say a child has composed a new piece of writing. Constructivist teachers first look back at previous writing and compare what the child has figured out in the new writing. Maybe there are fewer spelling errors. Perhaps the child has added more punctuation than previously. They might be making those big round periods to show they are newly aware of where their sentences end.

We are ready to consider the fundamental question that constructivist teachers ask themselves: What is the next logical concept this child needs to know to move their writing skills along? What is reasonable for this child? What will help them continue to make progress in their writing? What will help motivate them to see themselves as a writer? It could be character development. You determine that this child appears ready to add more details about the story's characters. This is the point when a curriculum is helpful. You can choose some lessons on character development.

DOI: 10.4324/9781032707921-3

You can put together a small group of students who all appear to be ready to work on their story's characters. The curriculum doesn't tell us *when* the child is ready – that is the teacher's job. The curriculum provides instructional resources to accommodate the skills you know your children are ready to tackle.

Let's explore the necessity for understanding child development. Putting the child's development first is essential rather than letting only the curriculum dictate how and what we teach. If we don't start with child development, we can get off track and lose our way, making learning harder for our children.

The American Question: Can We Ignore Development? (Dana)

Jean Piaget, the Swiss psychologist famous for his work on child development, would say that he became reluctant to speak to American audiences because he continued to get asked what he called *the American question*. What was the American question? This reoccurring question was about what stage of development American children should begin formal academics and whether American children develop at a different rate than other children worldwide. Therefore, they could start formal academics early – in the preoperational stage.

This idea propelled David Elkind, an American who studied under Piaget, to write his landmark book *The Hurried Child*. Elkind, Professor of Child Studies at Tufts University, saw Americans exposing their children to undue pressures of getting ahead. He said that we are miseducating young children "when we ignore what the child has to learn and instead impose what we want to teach, we put young children at risk for no purpose (p. 7)."

Many countries begin formal reading instruction at age 7 or 8. Piaget clarified that starting this formal instruction too early has long-lasting effects on children and how they perceive themselves as learners. So, we wonder, what makes Americans wish to ignore this deeply studied research? Why do we think our children develop differently and at a different rate than children in other parts of the world?

A widely publicized longitudinal study at Vanderbilt University studied the effect of a new program in 2015. Prekindergarten students were recruited for a large-scale academic pre-K program for low-income children in Tennessee. These new pre-K classrooms were designed to introduce academics sooner to "close the achievement gap while raising achievement for all learners."

The long-term results of the study are staggering. Compared with other students in the state not attending these preschools, the graduates of the academic preschools did better on academic tests in first grade. However, the differences faded over time, and by third grade, students in the program were performing worse than the others in every measure in the study – including reading, math, and even social and emotional measures. By sixth grade, the academic pre-K program graduates were significantly behind the others in academics, demonstrating more learning disabilities, rule violations, and behavior issues.

Is it possible that pushing formal academics onto young children creates less learning progress and more learning problems? The Vanderbilt study confirms what developmental psychologists have been telling us all along. Pushing children before they are ready results in less learning and development. Further, young children assume that if an adult expects them to be able to do something that they cannot do, then the problem is them. The children blame themselves. They question their abilities and may assume they are not smart. In education, we place them into special classes and groups with labels, making it clear they are behind the other children. They may begin to resent school and teachers or feel rebellious toward school authorities. They want out.

Constructivist theory proposes that formal academics should not begin until after the preoperational stage, at about age 7. That is not to say that we don't teach language and math in pre-K, kindergarten, and first grade, but we do so in a way that feels more like play. We introduce a rich literacy curriculum with much room for exploration and growth and less focus on mastery. This means much fewer "high stakes" assessment measures with the purpose of sorting students into groups of 'haves' and 'have nots'. Our instruction is developmentally appropriate.

A developmental approach helps children find the love of learning first. We can do less testing on young children and more independent work on projects the children are interested in exploring. We spend less time on reading worksheets and more time reading and sharing good books. The children can explore numbers and number concepts with engaging manipulatives and plenty of ordinary objects to discover shapes and sizes.

We teach with rhymes and songs and poetry. The children learn and play outside. (They should play outside a lot!) In these crucial primary grades, we ensure that opportunities to use oral language skills for authentic purposes are abundant throughout the day. For example, we can have short class meetings to consider topics relevant to our class, such as, "What should we have for a snack?" Or, "Let's make a birthday card for the principal." Maybe we plan how to celebrate having a new student in our class or find a solution to a problem the class has been experiencing.

Children should help maintain the classroom organization and set the table for snacks and celebrations. And, yes, they should rest. (Why did rest time become such an issue? Do we no longer have time for outside play and rest?) In all of these ways, children build a foundation for learning and a disposition to love learning.

Example for the American Question: Can We Ignore Development?

We all have an idea about when children should be able to do certain things. We tend to compare when children learn to walk. The average time for children to begin to walk is one year. The reality is that there is a wide gap in when babies take their first steps. Some children walk very early, at 7 or 8 months. Some children begin walking at 15 or 16 months. We may compare these milestones, but we don't tend to do anything about early or late walkers. We just let it happen. (No "Hooked on Walking" for our babies!) It is developmental. We tend to know the general sequence of development – in the case of walking, first, they turn over on their tummies, pull up onto their knees and crawl, cruise around furniture, and then take their first steps.

However, when children are near school age, we often forget about development and think more about what is expected by grade level. We may think that all kindergarteners should know how to write their names and identify letters and sounds. First graders should be reading, and all second graders should know how to tell time. Each of those skills and thousands of other skills children learn in school are developmental. Children learn these many skills in a predictable order *but at their own pace.*

Some children take a long time to learn the letters of the alphabet but may remember the many sounds associated with them quickly. Some children learn to subtract in third or fourth grade. The key is what we do to support their individual time frame without giving them the idea that something is wrong.

The study from Vanderbilt points out that starting academics sooner for some children not only has no effect but also has the potential for significant damage. We may have interfered with their need for time to learn, their belief in themselves, and how they see themselves as learners.

Primary schools focused solely on academics, ignoring development, run the risk of taking away a child's most important skill – the faith in themselves that they can do anything if they are allowed to do it at their own pace. Once that faith is taken away, it isn't easy to restore.

Questions for the American Question: Can We Ignore Development?:

◆ What is at the heart of *the American question,* this idea that our children should be able to do things sooner and better than other children in the world?

◆ Where do you find children being "hurried," as David Elkind describes in his landmark book *The Hurried Child*?

◆ Many educators approach primary instruction with students in less affluent schools or school districts as needing a more intense focus on academics. Have you seen this in your school district? What may be the result of this approach?

Looking at Students as Individuals: Child Development 101 (Dana)

Constructivists understand child development and Piaget's work in this area as the hallmark of his many educational contributions. Yet, our profession is still full of misunderstandings about child development. Most American schools consider what a child should know by grade level, but grade levels have little to do with how a child develops.

My mother made this mistake. The summer before I entered kindergarten, she discovered that I didn't know how to skip, and she thought all children should be able to skip before they enter kindergarten. To rectify the situation, she entered me in a dance class. It turns out I loved to dance, but I still couldn't skip. Luckily, they allowed me to enroll in kindergarten with this deficiency (and likely more). Skipping, it turns out, develops at about age 6 – toward the end of the preoperational stage. I was still 4 when I was enrolled in kindergarten.

My skipping example is not a unique situation. There needs to be more understanding of child development in our profession. As a kindergarten teacher, parents frequently asked me what skills or information their children needed before they came to school. Should they know the entire alphabet, be able to tie their shoes independently, or know how to write their names? School boards of education make this mistake as well. Many schools incorporate policies like requiring students to be able to read by the end of first grade or to be reading at a given reading level before they are allowed to move on to the next grade level.

Many states and school districts have adopted controversial poli-cies mandating reading on grade level by the end of third grade.

So, let us take a step back and examine child development from Jean Piaget's work. I like to introduce Piaget's stages of child development to teachers by addressing one question for each stage: *How is the child learning about their world at this stage?*

Please note that the ages associated with each stage are approximate.

The Sensorimotor Stage from Birth to about Age 2

This first stage of development is precisely what the name implies. Children in the sensorimotor stage learn their world through their senses and motor (movement) exploration. They touch, feel, move, drop, and put everything into their mouths. It is incredible information, and it lasts a lifetime. As an adult, you no longer need to drop your keys to see what they will do because you likely dropped keys from your high chair hundreds of times to see if they did the same thing after each drop. (And you also expected someone to pick them up each time.) At this stage, everything goes into the mouth, but that record of informa-tion can be found in the brain many years later. So you don't need to taste the metal frame of a chair. You know what it tastes like.

Interestingly, children in this stage love to try to move heavy things around. They are exploring how heavy items are to move. They will rearrange your living room without being asked. But the adult often tries to stop this learning by saying, "Don't pick that up. It's too heavy for you." I think the baby must be think-ing, "How do I know it's too heavy?"

The Preoperational Stage from about Age 2 to about Age 7

Children in this most exciting and frustrating stage learn about their world by associating names with items and grouping them with labels and categories. I call it a frustrating stage because having a need and not having the words to make that need known to someone who can fulfill it is frustrating. It is equally frustrating to see a child trying to communicate with you, but you can't understand what he is trying to say.

"Everything has a name." Helen Keller's teacher Ann said to her. (The movie *The Miracle Worker*, based on Helen Keller's life as a blind and deaf child, is worth watching as you think more about putting labels on things and placing them into groups.) Everything has a name, which means there are many things to learn. There are so many things to organize in the brain so that they can be retrieved when needed. Research tells us that children usually need many experiences with a new item along with someone to supply the label to get it placed in the brain. This is at the heart of why children who come to school with fewer experiences may appear to be behind others who have had more experiences. These children have more labels for items and more developed schema, or "file folders," meaning broader categories in their brains due to those experiences.

The Concrete Operational Stage from about Age 7 to about Age 11

To Piaget, operations are processes – such as rules, steps to follow, or guidelines. Children know their world with operations, and a child in this stage of development loves to learn them. Things like addition, subtraction, multiplication, punctuation rules, and rules on the playground. Some people call this the "military stage" because children at this stage like to learn one process at a time, get proficient at it, and then add another. They like rules. Standing on the playground, you can quickly tell who has begun this stage. The child constantly running to you to report another child breaking the rules has likely just moved into the concrete operational stage. Just a few weeks ago, they may have been preoperational and ignored all of the rules themselves, but suddenly, they have become the playground police, reporting every infraction.

Another tip for locating a new concrete operational child is to check with the librarian. Ask who is checking out the joke and riddle books. To get a joke is a new learning for concrete operational children. This is brain development. To get a joke is sophisticated work in the brain that requires, for the first time, the child to communicate with both sides of their brain – the right and left. Hear a joke in the left brain, create a picture of the action on the right, and apply the punchline back to the left. This communication in the brain's corpus callosum has grown and now functions where before it just wasn't up and running. A physical change has occurred.

The Formal Operational Stage from about Age 12 to Adult

Piaget called formal operations the "new thinking." You can consider another's perspective in this stage for the first time. You can understand that someone nice to you in person may say something bad about you behind your back. You can reason and think in the abstract. Logic is the key.

Suddenly, this child wants to take on causes and issues. They want to recycle everything, have fair laws, or make big judgments. They have opinions about everything. This may sound all too familiar for those raising teens. Their peers are more important than anyone, and they want to debate everything. But not all of us reach formal operations. Many factors influence who becomes formally operational and who does not, depending on experiences and the ability to reason and think logically.

Example for Looking at Students as Individuals: Child Development 101

One day, I decided to record myself conducting Piaget's conservation tasks with a child to use in professional development sessions. I could show teachers what these simple tools look like when used with a child. I asked a colleague if I could make a videotape of her son, Daniel, who was 4 years old at the time, the perfect age to show the delightful characteristics of a preoperational child.

As a quick reminder, Piaget devised seven conservation tasks to see how children process information. The first of the seven is the conservation of numbers (Figure 2.1). You ask the child to hold onto or conserve the concept of number even when it changes visually. A preoperational child will lose track of the number concept when the information visually changes. It is the brain connection that was discussed in the previous section.

To conduct the test, lay out eight of the same objects – coins, tiles, or small blocks – in two equally spaced rows. Establish that one row belongs to the child and the other is yours. Ask the child if the rows have the same number. Once you have established that the rows are the same, say, "Now I'm going

STEP 1 – Conservation Task

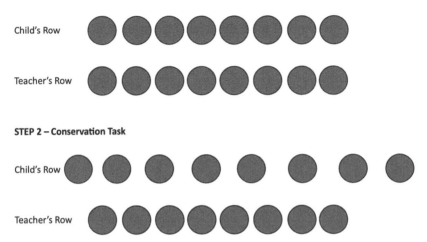

FIGURE 2.1 Conservation Task with Daniel

to change your row. Watch what I do." Move the child's row of objects to have more space between them to make it longer. Then, ask, "Now, do we have the same number?" The preoperational child cannot hold onto or conserve the concept of numbers and thinks they have more because the row has changed visually.

Daniel was so charming on the tape. He was a star. When I asked him if our rows were still the same, he hesitated and looked carefully, but after much consideration, he decided his row was more. That is not surprising for a 4-year-old.

A year later, I made another video with Daniel, now 5 years old and in kindergarten. I conducted the same task with the same result. Daniel was still not conserving.

I showed the first tape to educators in a professional development session. After the first tape, I asked the teachers to discuss what they had seen in small groups. Then I told them I had another video of Daniel a year later. I asked them to make a prediction. Would Daniel be able to conserve numbers on the second tape? Almost all of the educators predicted he would. They reasoned that he was so close at age 4, so bright and charming. The teachers were shocked when I showed them Daniel at age 5 – still unable to conserve numbers. They asked if he was unhappy, had a trauma, or had a family issue that caused him not to be able to do the task.

My question to the teachers in my sessions was, why would they expect a 5-year-old to be concrete operational? Maybe they saw a bright and social little boy and lost track of his development. What other factors can cause us to assume children are further along in their development than they are? This is why understanding child development is so important.

Questions for Looking at Students as Individuals: Child Development 101:

- ♦ When observing children, what can we learn about development and readiness?
- ♦ What do you tell parents who ask what their child needs to know before they enroll in kindergarten?
- ♦ Does your math curriculum first teach the rules and procedures? How should it change for preoperational children?
- ♦ How can we work to consider child development as we plan for student learning?
- ♦ We all make assumptions about student's level of development, and sometimes our assumptions are off base. What should we do next?

REFLECTION BOX B

What questions do you have for

LOOKING AT STUDENTS AS INDIVIDUALS: CHILD DEVELOPMENT 101?

Considering Children's Social and Emotional Development (Dana)

So many of our discussions are about the curriculum, math, and literacy, and some talk about social studies and science. I find myself thinking about children's social and emotional development too. Does it need to feel as if it is one or the other? Can we do both at the same time?

During school visits, I often see students sitting at desks or tables working on a computer or iPad. I hear about requirements for children to complete a certain amount of time or tasks on computer programs. But they don't appear to be very engaged and look sort of zoned out. I can't help but think, what about their social and emotional development? I observed no interactions between the students while they were working and only a few interactions with the teacher. What are they learning? Are they working on skills? Or how to sit quietly? I suppose, but beyond that, I'm not sure.

Teachers need to facilitate social and emotional development throughout the day. When an egocentric kindergartener wants to be the first child in the line to leave the room, and it is another child's turn, the teacher is there to help remind them that it is not their turn but will be soon. When two students fuss over a writing tool, the teacher can facilitate the negotiations to come to an agreement.

Class meetings have become another tool for developing social and emotional development. A few minutes, depending on the age of the students, at the beginning and again at the end of the day is a wonderful practice to foster social and emotional development. Consider a simple formula that can be adjusted for different or unique situations. For example, spend the first few minutes conducting a "check-in" with each student. Say the child's name and ask, "How are you today?" Or, "How are you feeling?" Children will learn, with consistency, to expand their responses, and you can encourage them by asking for clarification and using wait time to help them develop their thoughts before speaking.

Plan one short topic for the next phase of the class meeting. Select a topic that is both relevant and timely to the students. For example, an excellent place to start is an issue on the playground, a student in the school who had a breakthrough, a special occasion for a family, or an event on the news. Keep it short and to the point. For example: "I know you heard that the Perez family has a new baby this week." Then, ask a short, open-ended question such as, "How do you think things may have changed since the new baby came home?"

These types of discussions allow you to help students listen to others and prepare their responses. Keep this discussion short, 3 to 5 minutes, and avoid making it a lecture for you to provide students with your ideas. Make these discussions about the children expressing their thoughts and building on the ideas of their peers.

I like to end a morning class meeting by asking the students about their plans for the day or a class meeting at the end of the day by asking about their plans for the following school day. Children are seldom allowed or encouraged to express their plans, but it is invaluable. They will likely never think about their goals and plans if they are never asked about them. When asked consistently, students begin considering their plans and are likelier to follow through.

Academic subjects can also be an opportunity to help a child's social and emotional development. Can teaching reading and writing be connected to a child's social and emotional development? Of course. It is in the conversations. In her landmark book *Conversations*, Regie Routman (1999) has written extensively about a developmental approach to reading instruction. She suggests helping students make personal connections to authors and texts. In this way, children connect what is known and personal to learning about others' lives and cultures. She uses literature to foster independence, helping each child offer their unique voice and perspective when having collaborative conversations about books.

According to Routman, using literature helps students love classroom conversations because each student gets to be heard. Conversations about literature can set a great feeling tone for the classroom, and various texts can help the class develop a sense of shared experience and community. She stresses the importance of having critical literacy conversations and going deep on real-life issues and struggles. This in-depth conversation leads to higher levels of comprehension in addition to a better understanding of life's unique problems.

Social and emotional development is foundational to creating a classroom environment conducive to learning. Let's look closely at our learning day and ensure that we consider children's social and emotional development in many ways throughout the day, not just for 30 minutes for social-emotional learning, and then we go back to "real life."

Example for Considering Children's Social and Emotional Development

I had the opportunity to visit and work in England during two different school terms over two years. Of all the interesting things I learned from this experience, the process of serving lunch intrigued me. As I consider social and emotional development, I recall that the British schools I visited had a system for serving lunch that was an excellent example of prioritizing three fundamental social skills: sharing, taking turns, and serving others.

Lunch in these English schools is called *dinner* and is served at round tables that seat about ten students. Round tables are ideal for conversation and community. I can't imagine what the teachers at this school would think about our commonplace American cafeteria tables – long, rectangular, fold-up tables with benches for seats. These tables don't allow for quality communication. Not to mention, children struggle with staying seated because the benches are often an awkward size for them. They are wrong for so many reasons.

And here is the real shocker when I think about how different the dinner is organized in these English schools: They eat in mixed-age groups. In other words, they don't fill the entire lunchroom space with same-age students. A cafeteria filled with kindergarteners can be a recipe for disaster, where it can be hard for much social or emotional development to take place.

Our American schools' lunchrooms are often too loud, hectic, or silent. Neither meets our goal. They can be stressful for the children and the adults. In England, the table of ten was organized with two of the oldest students as "Dinner Captains," along with about four middle age students (8- to 10-year-olds) and four of the youngest children (ages 5 to 7).

The Dinner Captains, the oldest children in the school, oversee the table. Food is served family style, and the Dinner Captains make sure the platters are passed in the correct direction and that each child takes an appropriate amount of food. Beyond just the process of passing food, the Dinner Captains also managed the behavior at the table. They set the tone for the conversation, steering the little ones away from inappropriate topics, keeping their voices at an conversational level, using table manners – all of the things we don't teach in lunchrooms enough. They used real tableware, not plastic, and were expected to stay at the table, eat, and converse with the others. They are sharing and taking turns.

The Dinner Captains are learning to serve others with a safety net of the school system as a backup to help support them if they need help. About every two weeks, a teacher met with the Dinner Captains to discuss their efforts and helped them with strategies for any issues they encountered. Here, the Dinner Captains aired their complaints and frustrations. They discussed how to keep the younger children on the right path appropriately. It was so interesting to hear this meeting of 11- and 12-year-olds who would be doing some of the very things they are complaining about themselves if they had not been put into this position of authority.

Within this system for daily school lunches, the younger students have role models for their social and emotional development – older students that they look up to. Middle age students begin to consider when they will become Dinner Captains, and the oldest students take this responsibility very seriously. They are truly learning to serve others. Furthermore, the adults can move from table to table to encourage and support children without the typical stress of monitoring the lunchroom.

Questions for Considering Children's Social and Emotional Development:

◆ Do you plan for social and emotional development just like in other areas like math, language, and social studies? If not, how can you add more to your school day?
◆ Do math, reading, and other subject areas offer opportunities for social and emotional development?

♦ How much time are your students spending on screen time? Is it taking away from their social and emotional development? What can you do to change that if you answered "yes"?

♦ How can you facilitate productive conversations with students and give them many opportunities for conversations throughout the school day?

REFLECTION BOX C

What questions do you have for

CONSIDERING CHILDREN'S SOCIAL AND
EMOTIONAL DEVELOPMENT?

Allowing Children to Fail: Who Is Really Responsible? (Dana)

Constructivists allow children to fail. I know that sounds harsh, maybe even un-American, but it is so true and has many implications for how children learn, set goals, and find accomplishments in their future. We all need to fail to learn how to recover and move forward. School is the perfect place to make mistakes. School becomes the safety net for students to make mistakes before they get to the real world, where mistakes have more significant consequences. *But what if their failure is due to our unrealistic goals for them?*

This may be the more complicated truth; some children may fail because we have put unrealistic expectations on them. Reading instruction is a good example. I hear about schools that expect children to read by a specific grade level. Some schools say all kindergarteners will be reading by the end of their kindergarten year, all first graders will be reading at a certain level, and all children will read at grade level by third grade. Is that possible? Or the real question is, why would we do that? Why do we need to have all children at the same level at the same time? I propose we do this because it is easier for schools and a way to determine who will succeed and who will fail.

Let's be realistic. In kindergarten, the range of development is huge. One child may have just turned 5 years old, while another has been 6 for months – a large span coupled with differences in experiences, interests, and social and emotional development. Having the entire class of kindergarteners at the same level may sound like a teacher's dream, but one of the most significant factors of child development and learning is having peers who are just above your development do something interesting you haven't figured out how to do yet.

We know the span for learning to read is very wide. You may have known a 4-year-old who taught themselves how to read, but most children figure it out between ages 6 to 8. Many European schools don't even teach formal reading until the age of 7 or 8. If we expect children to read long before they are ready to figure it out, we may set them up for failures that are hard to correct later. We put them into special classes, label them with disabilities, and, worst of all, retain them because we had the wrong expectations.

When students fail, constructivist teachers monitor progress and change our approach to help students succeed. We know them as learners, so we know where they are and what the next logical step would be for individual learners to help them increase their learning and levels of success. For example, children may need to be placed into small, targeted groups for intervention with other children who have about the same skill set. Those groups are valuable for short periods at a time – about 20 minutes and should be done so that children do not feel as if they are going out of the classroom with another teacher because they have failed. The sessions should be focused on practice by giving children tools for supporting their development right where they are. Ideally, they should be done in their classroom rather than pulled out of the classroom. After completing an evaluation and the child exhibits success, they should be discontinued.

You learn to read first by hearing someone you admire read a good book aloud, and you think, "I want to be able to do that too." That is called a *disposition*, which was addressed in Chapter 1. Marie Clay's (2001) research in New Zealand demonstrated that if a child hears a book read aloud for about 15 minutes a day from birth until they enter school, most are bound to be readers by around age 8. It seems so simple to listen to books read by a caring adult, and you are interested enough to want to learn to read. Once you have developed the disposition, you have it for life.

So what about the children who come to us without having heard 15 minutes of reading daily? We have to make up for all of those good books. We must develop that disposition by reading many books to them. Reading five books aloud daily will add up to about 500 books by the holiday break, and the children gain those important literacy experiences in school.

Failures will happen, and children need to make mistakes to learn, but let's not set them up for failure. If an administration declares that all students must achieve a given level of skill all at the same time using this in order to pass or fail them, we are running the risk of a label and a failure that is with a child throughout their school career and beyond.

Example for Allowing Children to Fail: Who Is Really Responsible?

My dear friend and neighbor Mary and I used to go for long walks and talk about school, family, and life. Mary was a wonderful preschool teacher for a local school district.

On one of our walks, Mary told me about a meeting she and her husband had with the local elementary school about her son, Marcus, who was early into the second grade. Marcus's teacher was concerned that he was not yet reading. The teacher had asked the special reading teacher to do some diagnostic testing with Marcus, and they both met with Mary and Frank and suggested that they may want to put Marcus into a special reading class. It would be a pull-out program where Marcus would meet daily with a small group of students at about the same reading level in a separate classroom down the hallway.

Mary's response to this suggestion is one I have always remembered and shared with teachers hundreds of times. Mary said, "You know what, I don't think we want to do that yet because, here's the thing, Marcus doesn't know he can't read, and I don't want to do anything that would give him the idea something may be wrong with him."

Marcus started reading about midway through his second-grade year. Mary and Frank continued to read him books and encourage his various interests. A special reading class may have helped him figure out some things about reading, but it may have also done what Mary was concerned about. We don't have a crystal ball to tell us when a child is developmentally ready to learn something new, like reading. We must figure out how to support a student in their journey without taking away their "can-do" attitude. And, at all costs, we should avoid making decisions about a child by comparing them to other children. Development is just too unique for that ever to work.

By the way, Marcus graduated high school and went on to university, where he graduated with a degree in journalism. He is a sportswriter for a major newspaper, and I doubt anyone is concerned that he didn't read until second grade.

BOX D Literature Connections for the Classroom

Check out these favorite children's books that demonstrate how kids can learn from failure, develop in their own time, and believe they can.

Abdul's Story
by Jamilah Thompkins-Bigelow and Tiffany Rose
Abdul is a storyteller who struggles with writing. He learns how to write his beautiful words anyway.

Beautiful Oops
by Barney Saltzberg
For the kids who rip up their mistakes, so many possibilities await as a result of a mistake.

Thank You, Mr. Falker
by Patricia Polacco
Patricia Polacco's biographical account of a wonderful teacher, Mr. Falker, who helped her learn to read and believe in herself.

The Girl Who Never Made Mistakes
by Mark Pett and Gary Rubinstein
Beatrice Bottomwell doesn't fail. And she never makes mistakes. Until one day, she makes a colossal mistake!

The Magical Yet
by Angel DiTerlizzi and Lorena Alvarez Gomez
Yet, the magical word that tells us it's okay if we can't do something we yearn to do...yet.

The Thing Lou Couldn't Do
by Ashley Spires
Lou is brave and adventurous and afraid of heights. Her friends help Lou face her fear step by step.

When Things Aren't Going Right, Go Left
by Marc Colaggiovanni and Peter Reynolds
When a boy experiences worry and fear, he leaves them behind and learns to manage things not going right by going left.

Questions for Allowing Children to Fail: Who Is Really Responsible?:

♦ Do we have realistic or unrealistic goals for when students should have accomplished a skill?
♦ Are we communicating failure to students without considering how it may affect them?
♦ What are the long-term effects of failure on students?
♦ What are your concerns about schools using set markers for determining failure?

REFLECTION BOX E

What questions do you have for

ALLOWING CHILDREN TO FAIL: WHO IS REALLY RESPONSIBLE?

High and Low: What Do We Mean When We Call Children "Low" or "High"? (Krista)

Once we understand child development and believe that children should only be compared to themselves, we have another development issue to address. Is the way we talk about students reflecting these beliefs? We often hear children referred to as academically "high" or "low" in schools. There are "high" reading and math groups and "low" reading and math groups. "Low" students are often referred for more assessment. "Low" students are added to intervention groups for additional instruction. "High" students are referred to gifted programs. "Low" students are considered for retention. "High" students often receive more opportunities for engaging projects, extracurricular activities, and special classes.

Constructivist teachers are willing to have the conversation where they examine what we mean when we refer to students as "low." Do we mean that the child is behind? Low achievement? Low ability? Low level of engagement? Maybe the time has come to drop the term "low" when referring to children and their abilities. For that matter, let's consider dropping the term "high" too. Here is why.

I think students usually know if teachers believe they are "high" or "low." I spend my days working with the students who are regularly called "low." Yet, I see them grow as readers and thinkers, writers, speakers, and listeners every day – often catching up to the learning expectations over time with lessons planned specifically for them.

So, if these students are growing and learning, why do we call them "low"? Because they haven't met the set benchmark for their grade? Even though their age, amount of school, development, learning experiences, and learning process may be different, in school, we often use a grade-level benchmark to describe a child's innate ability (rather than as a measure of progress on a certain aspect of learning).

What about our growth mindset as teachers? Much has been written recently about teaching children to have a growth mindset and attribute their failures and successes to their effort and persistence. As teachers, we can also work with a growth mindset about our children and know that they may need more learning experiences and time to learn a new skill or sort out their confusion with a concept. It does not mean they don't have the ability. Just not yet.

I am concerned about what being called "low" does to children and their beliefs about their inherent worth and ability to learn hard things. When a child is believed to be "low," does it make us work harder to help the child become "average" and then "high"? Or does it resign the teacher to a belief that once they are "low," they are always "low"?

It feels like we have seen both scenarios play out multiple times. A struggling student gets a highly effective teacher who believes in each child's potential, and they grow in their learning. Sometimes, this is treated as a "miracle" at the school – "Look how well 'so-and-so' is doing! Isn't it a miracle?!" (Yet we know a skilled teacher is behind that miraculous growth.) Or a child gets a minimally effective teacher, and they continue to slide down the achievement scale only to end up further behind than before.

A teacher with a growth mindset believes each child can grow under their instruction. This constructivist teacher believes they can affect the child's learning, emotional, and academic success. We also believe that we can grow and learn as professionals. We can continue to improve at understanding the learning needs of students who struggle or learn differently in our classrooms.

In American schools, as we are now pushing the reading curriculum down to kindergarten, I have found that more and more children are labeled as behind and referred to as "low." I've often seen the students referred to as "low" as children who just need more time to learn. If they get a series of proactive primary teachers who pick up where the last left off, meeting the children where they are, often the students can gain a lot of ground in their reading through first and second grade. Others may have a learning disability, and they need a teacher skilled in learning disabilities to help them understand and grow.

Grade levels are delineated by a grade-level curriculum, for sure. However, these grade-level curricula overlap, and there is room for value-added learning in each school year. Value-added learning is when children's learning is enhanced by instructional efforts to individualize lessons to the learner's specific needs, resulting in more than average growth during that time. If the teacher believes that children can grow as learners, not resigned to being "low" learners for life, children can thrive in school. For example, when a big-box curriculum is employed in the school, it rarely meets the unique learning needs of a struggling student. This is when children need an astute teacher who can offer individualized planning, instruction, and monitoring of growth in learning.

As for children referred to as "high," learning problems can also occur; these students often see themselves as innately smart and assume all learning should come easily. They do not know how to ask for help when learning is hard. Their parents may assume they never need help and do not know how to help them. These students may shut down and just try to get past the content they do not understand and move on. As the child grows into more difficult curricula, they may have emotional and academic consequences if they do not learn how to persevere through challenging content. Everyone expects them to do well in school, and when they fail, it is hard to know what went wrong in the learning process.

We hear stories every day of people who became successful despite having a damaging school experience where teachers did not believe in their abilities. Moreover, we also hear stories every day of people who had a teacher who believed they could, and they did. These examples make the case for educators to look at each child as a learner with a repertoire of strengths and needs – not "high," not "low," or even "average." Just unique learners who are on a path of learning supported by teachers who meet them where they are.

An Example for High and Low: What Do We Mean When We Call Children "Low" or "High"?

Teachers' meetings, grade level meetings, and teacher-to-teacher conversations about students inevitably have excessive references to children being "high" or "low" at one academic subject or another – or generally them all. It's hard to avoid those words. As a reading specialist, you know what my students are called. I am often pulled aside by a teacher to be told about a "low" student in their class whom I should probably be working with. So, I've developed a list of general follow-up questions in this situation. I start with, "What is their name? And what's their birthday?" Then, "Is she/he learning English?" "How has his/her attendance been?" And, "Have you spoken with a parent to learn about the child?" Then I move to, "What did you notice when you read with them?" Or, "What do you notice about their speaking, listening, writing, motivation, … engagement?" "What are this child's strengths?" "What do you see as the most urgent learning needs?"

I am not always met with much information, but my questions start the conversation by addressing the child as an individual we need to get to know and then discover their specific learning strengths and needs.

Questions for High and Low: What Do We Mean When We Call Children "Low" or "High"?:

♦ When do you hear children referred to as "low" or "high"?
♦ What can you do to support students referred to as "low" or "high" in your classroom, grade level, and school?
♦ How can you help reframe the word "low" about children in your workplace? How about "high" or "average"?
♦ If the terms "low" or "high" were dropped from your school's vocabulary, what might that do for the school climate and community?

REFLECTION BOX F

What questions do you have for

HIGH AND LOW- WHAT DO WE MEAN WHEN WE CALL CHILDREN "HIGH" and "LOW"?

The Heart of Child Development

Constructivists always consider the child's development. Development means comparing each child only to themselves. We use instructional benchmarks as general guides, not markers of success or failure, making sure to monitor the progress and growth of each child. If a child is not making progress, we adjust our practices. Constructivist teachers understand that development goes beyond the early childhood years and continues into school age and teens – considering how each child is advancing in their social, cognitive, and language development. In this way, children inform us as teachers to adopt developmentally appropriate practices for each child in our classroom.

3

One at a Time, All at Once

How does your class operate? Constructivist teachers have a "one at a time, all at once" mindset. We view the classroom as a children's workshop. The room is set up with the child at the heart. As the days, weeks, and months go by, the classroom remains a child's space where we learn, grow, make mistakes, make friends, and become a community of learners.

The constructivist teacher works with each child, sometimes individually, sometimes in small groups, and sometimes all together. The class moves in and out of groups as the learning focus changes throughout the day. How does this work? What needs to happen to make the classroom this type of children's workshop? In Chapter 3, we consider classroom spaces, materials, choice, projects, and how we teach. We start with a balanced schedule.

A Balanced Schedule (Dana)

We often look at our daily schedule as adult-driven and dictated by the school's master schedule, with set times like arrival, lunch, special classes, and recess dictated for each grade level. This can make us feel as though we have little say in our schedules, yet we can be purposeful and creative with the time the children are with us.

DOI: 10.4324/9781032707921-4

We can create a balanced schedule that considers the day from the child's point of view. The entire day can be organized by how each activity feels to the students. Some parts of the day feel as if the teacher is in control. I call this time whole-group, teacher-directed instruction. Typically, all the students are gathered in a space where their attention can be directed to the speaker. In many primary classrooms, whole-group instruction is delivered with students seated on the carpet and the teacher sitting in front of them.

Small-group instruction is delivered to about four to six children, often seated around a small table where the teacher can hear and interact with each child. Reading and math lessons are often presented in small groups in the early primary classroom. While one group works with the teacher, the rest of the classroom may work in independent small groups, such as with partners or individually.

Independent small-group time may include work at learning centers. Students can be assigned work at learning centers or choose from a list of possible centers. Individual work may include hands-on reading, math, writing, or inquiry activities.

How each of these times is structured and where they are placed in the schedule will dictate how the schedule feels to the students. Some teachers arrange their schedule so that all intense subjects are first in the day while students are fresh. Others want a "soft opening" with a more casual feel to the beginning of the day before the real learning begins.

Here is how I approach a balanced schedule. I want to balance teacher-directed times with child-directed times throughout the day. For example, if I begin the day with a whole-group read aloud, I will balance that time by following with a child-directed activity – back and forth between teacher directed and child directed. The key is how it feels to the child. Listening to someone talking feels long. Getting to talk or follow your own interests feels like time flies. Whole-group, teacher-directed time is valuable and necessary, but it cannot go too long. If students have had to listen too long, you may be doing the best lesson, but no learning occurs. In primary classrooms, whole-group instruction will usually last from 10 to 20 minutes.

Here is a **sample** balanced schedule. What do you notice?

TABLE 3.1 Sample School Day Schedule

Activity	Type	Description	Time
Class Meeting	Whole Group	Teacher led but with ample time for students to talk and share ideas. Read aloud a story that fits the class meeting topic. Have a conversation in a circle.	15 minutes
Small-Group Reading and Learning Centers	Small-Group and Independent Small-Group Work	One small group meets with the teacher for 15 minutes while others work in their choice of learning centers.	60 minutes
Center Review Time	Whole Group	Teacher-led share session and review of learning that was completed. Students talk and may share their artifacts.	5–10 minutes
Word Study	Whole Group (5 min) Independent (15 min)	Introduce word study lesson. Children work independently with their own set of materials.	20 minutes
Recess	Independent	Children choose their preferred activity with teacher supervision.	15 minutes
Read Aloud	Whole Group	Teacher directed with students interacting in conversations about the book.	15 minutes
Writing	Whole Group (10 min) Small Group/ Independent (20 min) Whole-Group Share Time (5–10 minutes)	Start with a short read aloud and mini-lesson about what writers do. Students work on independent writing activities while the teacher works with individual students or small groups. Share time to present writing for the last 5–10 minutes.	40 minutes
Specials	May Vary Depending on How Each Teacher Structures the Time	It may be helpful in designing your schedule to consider how each special teacher structures his or her class to decide what to do afterward.	55 minutes

(Continued)

TABLE 3.1 (Continued)

Activity	Type	Description	Time
Independent Reading	Independent	Start with a short read aloud. Each child reads books from their own book boxes. Teacher helps students choose books, visits with students about their books, and listens in on their reading, making anecdotal notes.	15-30 minutes
Lunch	Independent	Depending on how the cafeteria is organized, this time may or may not feel like independent time.	30 minutes
Rest and Read Aloud	Whole Group	Teacher-led read aloud with quiet time for students to rest in a comfortable space.	10 minutes
Math Mini-Lesson	Whole Group	Teacher-led math lesson. May include a math read aloud and/or demonstration and shared practice.	15 minutes
Small-Group Math and Learning Centers	Small Group and Independent Small Group	One small group meets with the teacher for 15 minutes while others work in their choice of learning centers.	60 minutes
Recess	Independent	Children choose their preferred activity with teacher supervision.	15 minutes
Directions for Project Work	Whole Group	Teacher provides directions for a science or social studies project time.	10 minutes
Project Work	Small Group and Independent	Students work in small student-led groups or independently on a project that is ongoing for multiple days or weeks.	30 minutes
Review Project Work	Whole Group	Students share their small-group or independent work on their projects.	10 minutes
Prepare for the End of the Day	Independent	Each child gathers their materials, cleans workspaces, and prepares for dismissal.	10 minutes

Add up the minutes for each type of activity.

Whole Group: total number of minutes_____
Small Group: total number of minutes_____
Independent: total number of minutes_____

For the schedule to be balanced, the number of minutes spent in whole-group, teacher-directed time in a primary classroom should be less than that spent in small and independent groups. Try this out with your schedule.

Example for a Balanced Schedule

Two kindergarten teachers asked me to help them with some concerns with their students at the beginning of the day. I went to the school to observe the time as students arrived and stayed for the morning until we had time to talk. This classroom was structured with two teachers working with about 50 students in a double-sized classroom.

Here is what I observed: When children arrived, they were called to the large carpet area to sit on the floor for the calendar time. This teacher-directed time allowed very little opportunity for students to contribute or talk. One child at a time was called to the front of the group to move or add something to a large calendar display. What could have been completed in 10 minutes took much longer because of all the interruptions to correct behavior issues. Next, one of the teachers read a book aloud. Very little interaction was observed except for admonishing children for not paying attention, talking to another child, or even getting up from the group and leaving the carpet.

After that, a teacher did a phonics lesson on beginning sounds. Children were shown picture cards and asked to say in unison what the picture was and call out what sound they heard at the beginning. This activity lasted 15 minutes mainly because more time was spent correcting behavior. Finally, a teacher reviewed the schedule on a large chart and discussed what the students would be doing for the day. Again, this went on for more than

15 minutes. Much too long, and by now, almost no one was attending to what the teacher was saying, including me! Several students had left the area. Many were lying down – even though they had been told to sit up multiple times, and everyone appeared upset. An hour into their day, these kindergarteners were done.

Here is what the posted schedule included:

Calendar Time	10 minutes
Read Aloud	20 minutes
Phonics Lesson	15 minutes
Class Meeting	10 minutes

But each of those activities was whole-group teacher directed. When I pointed this out to them and discussed how to balance their schedule, the teachers began to discuss how the day felt to their students. Changes to the schedule were made, and after that, everything worked better for the teachers and their students.

Questions for a Balanced Schedule:

♦ How long do I spend in whole-group, teacher-directed time each day?

♦ When do I see my students needing to be more attentive during the day?

♦ What parts of my schedule allow my students to make choices about their work? How can I provide more opportunities for choice?

♦ Even during whole-group, teacher-directed time, am I allowing students to talk, share their experiences, and ask questions?

REFLECTION BOX A

What questions do you have for

A BALANCED SCHEDULE?

Classroom Spaces with Heart (Dana)

For me, classroom spaces with heart means designing the classroom for the students. When assigned a classroom, you get to design the space to work for the adults and the many young people who live and work together in the room. I love creating spaces for children. I have helped hundreds of teachers design classroom spaces and written a book on the subject.

First, I start with cleaning and purging. This comes from my mother. Twice a year (the beginning of spring and the beginning of fall), my mother had us pull out everything in our closet and remove anything we had not worn during that season. The same is true for our classrooms. Pull out storage cabinets with games, toys, materials, and supplies. If you didn't use something the previous year, you probably won't use it this year. Reorganize your storage spaces and find another home for items you don't use anymore.

Putting like things together is my mantra. It helps at home when we are looking for something, and we can do the same at school. The children can help sort the items. For example, glue is in the container labeled "glue" and stored on a shelf in the closet with other items used for similar purposes, such as tape and scissors. It makes sense to put the supplies for writing in the writing center. Have a tub of toys for recess stored near the coat closet, and put the puzzle shelf and math manipulatives in the math center. Children do better when the room is organized in a way they understand and can count on. It helps them think logically and helps with cleanup time.

Finally, I am a big fan of labeling. Early in my career, I saw some research about young children's visual memory, explaining that children have a better visual memory than adults. You know this if you've ever played a memory game with a young child. They can beat you even when you are trying very hard, and they look as if they are hardly paying attention. I decided to try it out by labeling the tubs in my learning centers. Could the children put things back in the right space if the materials were labeled? Yes, they can, and the added benefit is they also learn the words on the cards almost effortlessly. This is the power of visual memory. Hook up the printed word with a picture and the actual material, and you have secured that printed word in their brain.

Be thoughtful about how you label. Print the item's name in large letters and draw or print a picture of the item. Then make three labels: one for the front of the container, one for the back, and one on the shelf where the tub is to be located. I learned to put the one on the back because my students always managed to put the container on the shelf backward during cleanup time. Labeling takes time, but it is so worth it. You can start with areas where students have the most difficulty putting things back where they belong.

Make sure the space works for your students. If you have a chart with each student's picture and name printed beside it, students will know all their classmates' names and can recognize them in print. I would spend less time on premade design themes and less money on commercial décor or elaborate displays. You can leave bulletin boards blank until children's work can be displayed. This is a quick way to make every child feel at home and valued in the classroom. Start simply and introduce new materials when children need them. Constructivist teachers work to make the classroom organized in a child-centered way.

Example for Classroom Spaces with Heart

We can get multiple uses from some spaces. If you have a large carpet area for the whole-group, teacher-directed instruction, yet that space is empty other times throughout the day, give it an additional purpose. You can add bookshelves around the perimeter, and during center time, this area becomes the library center, a cozy space for reading books. Or add storage for games and make the space a game center where students can work in small groups on math or other games.

Consider how much time a space is used compared to how much space it takes in the classroom. If you have individual workspaces or desks for each child, consider how much time they are used throughout the day. Individual workspaces are often used only approximately 25% of the daily schedule but take up over

75% of the area in the room. When the ratio of use is out of balance in this way, you may want to consider other options for your space, such as using a flexible individual workspace. Maybe you want to allow students to pick the type of space that is best for them. Options may include low tables, pillows, and lapboards for working on the floor. Check how much space your teacher area is taking up in the classroom and consider how much you use your desk in relation to how much space it takes up in the room. A large adult desk may be too much.

Create a floor plan of your classroom, just like a designer would use, so you can "move furniture" without pushing heavy pieces around the room. Use grid paper where each square represents one square foot, and try out various floor plans considering traffic patterns, where plug-ins are located, and your sightlines from multiple vantage points.

You can place materials where they are used or where they make the most sense. Put a tub of individual whiteboards near the whole-group instructional area and include the dry-erase markers and erasers in a container nearby. Put the magnetic letters, sound boxes, small easel, teacher materials, and books for small-group instruction near your small-group instruction table. You get the idea.

Carefully consider the storage for the art center and writing center. For example, art paper should lay flat and have easy accessibility, and make sure many types of writing paper and writing utensils are available for student choice. You can place special pens and colored pencils in a small round container that allows students to select the one they need for their project. Add a large plastic tub for recycling odds and ends of paper and a display board near these centers for displaying children's center accomplishments. When you consider your classroom spaces, your day will run smoothly, the children will have ownership in taking care of the classroom, and you'll have more time for teaching and learning.

Questions for Classroom Spaces with Heart:

♦ What areas in your classroom feel cluttered or are difficult for the students to keep the way it was designed?

- Does your classroom space easily support whole-group, small-group, and individual learning?
- How could you rethink this space to help your students manage the materials better?
- Where would you start to add more labels to your materials?
- Is the room set up to be inviting and child-centered?

REFLECTION BOX B

What questions do you have for

SPACES WITH HEART?

Adapting Materials to a Constructivist Approach (Krista)

Constructivist teachers work to tailor lessons to student's current academic needs and interests. Yet, we don't need to develop every lesson plan from scratch each day. It would take hours and, I believe, take away from time for teaching and reflecting on student learning and next steps. So, we often rely on premade curricular materials. Some of these premade materials come in a "one-size-fits-all" big box with a lot of print materials. Other premade curricular materials are developed with a constructivist intent, and the curricular units offer options based on what students need.

Schools and school districts often choose the "big box" programs to ensure that all grade-level standards are taught and every teacher has what they need to teach the entire grade-level curriculum in their classroom. That's good because when we have high-quality materials, we have more time to plan our lessons based on what the children in our classroom need. Constructivist teachers are adept at taking these "one-size-fits-all" lesson materials and turning them into more individually focused activities and authentic lessons.

For example, a typical spelling lesson could become a phonemic awareness lesson. In this way, the students assemble each word with magnetic letters, and as they are assembling the words, the teacher can observe to see if children hear sounds in words and how they apply this knowledge to spelling. This type of lesson can go far beyond the original rote spelling list. Students can use each spelling word to create a word ladder, and so on.

A typical 30-problem math page could become a teamwork activity where student pairs pick a problem and show three different ways to solve it. Now, we have added divergent thinking, conversation, and choice.

So, how do teachers transform premade curricular materials to a constructivist approach? Here are six strategies to help teachers adapt almost any lesson or curricular material to a more engaged, personalized, and active learning approach.

1) **Adapt worksheets**. I am constantly surprised by how many worksheets students still do in school. Sometimes, even packets of worksheets! These can be adapted to a more meaningful learning activity. Try to always move the worksheet to the blank page in one form or another. You can get to the heart of the intended learning outcome through more authentic means. If it was fill-in-the-blank for vocabulary, change it to using the vocabulary in context on a sentence strip or making a vocabulary four square poster for the vocabulary word. You can reference those vocabulary sentence strips or four square model posters throughout the unit.

Instead of fill-in-the-blank, children can construct sentences on sentence strips. If you're working on grammar, cut up the sentences and ask children to put the sentences back together using language and grammar. Post the sentences on the wall for everyone to read.

I love to observe emergent and beginning readers work on cut-up sentences. I learn so much about their ability to look at words closely using their phonics and language skills simultaneously to reconstruct a sentence. This activity could be even better if the sentences were derived from the student's language about a text!

2) **Use manipulatives to help students understand the concept and visually "see" their thinking**. Are you working on phonics? Use magnetic letters, letter tiles, sound boxes, syllable tiles (blank or premade), two-column word sorts (or more columns!)

    Are you working on math? Use base ten blocks, interlocking cubes, colored counters/bears/beans.

    Are you working on geography? Use geography puzzles, make relief maps, and create geography cards.

    This also applies to reading, science, and every other subject. Students need a concrete representation to solidify their understanding before moving to more abstract representations.

    It is essential to make sure *every* child gets to use the manipulatives. I often see the lesson demonstrated with one set of manipulatives for the teacher, yet students rarely touch them. Or one set for a table, and four children get to share. I have found that my teaching is more successful when every child gets their own set of manipulatives to construct their own knowledge.

    Put sets of manipulatives in small Ziploc bags or plastic cups for each student. Now, they are ready for multiple uses and are easy to manage and gather by the students.

3) **Turn the activity into a game**. Children love games. Find ways to turn learning into a game in every content area. Even games where everyone can win. Play four corners where students go to the corner with the sign representing their point of view. Students can share their thoughts in their corner and then with the broader group to earn the classroom's "Great Thinkers" distinction.

    Many curriculum materials have games built in for paired and independent practice. Sometimes, teachers eliminate the games due to time constraints. It's important to keep the games in the curriculum. As best you can, try not to put teams of students against each other. Set a goal, and everyone who beats that goal wins. This keeps teams engaged and working, not quitting once another team wins.

It's important to note that we are not against children learning how to lose. It's important to learn how to deal with defeat. In the classroom, students will often stop trying when they know they can't win. More students will keep trying (and learning!) if they can meet a goal. (Some teams may not achieve the goal, but when competing against themselves, they are likelier to stay with the task.)

4) **Read or tell a story to bring the concept to life for students**. A story is meaningful, and we can remember it more easily. Why do children watch Disney movies repeatedly? Our brains are engaged, and we love a story to commit to memory. Use stories to make learning come alive in your classroom. For example, if you teach students how to write a sentence, a question, a statement, and an exclamation, use the story *Punctuation Takes a Vacation* by Robin Pulver to illustrate why the different punctuation marks are important to help us read and make meaning.

Here are some wonderful books that tell a story to make learning come to life. Use *The Word Collector* by Peter H. Reynolds to teach about vocabulary and multi-syllabic words. If you're teaching students to write fiction, read *Ralph Tells a Story* by Abby Hanlon to illustrate how we come up with stories and then start our own story. I love the classic *Six Dinner Sid* by Inga Moore as an introduction to number sense and multiplication. Using a story to teach concepts gives the skill a hook in the child's brain that we, as teachers, can refer to and help students access as they learn a new concept. Stories make historical facts and figures come alive. They stick in our memories. Of course, I've been known to make up a story to fit the concept I am trying to teach, and I'm guessing you might have done that too.

5) **Make it a project or mini-project**. When you need to check for student understanding, you could use the published end-of-unit test, but what if you adapted the final assessment to a project? You can develop a project or mini-project that students can create using their knowledge of

the content to demonstrate their learning. These projects and mini-projects take learning a step further, adding creativity, choice, and students' individual preferences to bring learning to higher levels of understanding.

Rather than reiterating knowledge level understanding, with a project, students can demonstrate the ability to compare, contrast, critique, analyze, or synthesize essential unit concepts. A project usually takes more than one day. An example of a project could be the development of a living history museum where each student chooses a historical figure, researches, writes a short biography, then dresses up as the figure and poses as that figure in the classroom-turned-living history museum. Other classes are invited to visit your living history museum.

Another project example would be to write a class How-To book by having each student publish a How-To essay with diagrams and then compile it into a class book. I've done this many times, and I am always tickled by the fact that I often have one or two students choose to write How to Drive. I require students to write about something they know well for their How-To essay, so I check in to ensure they can thoroughly describe driving. Yet, they always surprise me with an inexplicably in-depth knowledge of driving. (I wonder if their parents know how closely they are being watched in the car!)

When teaching measurement, a great project would be to measure the lunchroom, lunch tables, or gym. Report your results to the cafeteria crew or physical education teacher. Brainstorm ways this information could be helpful to them. Or, with older students, determine the square footage of the classroom or school. Then, make a report to the principal in case a carpet needs to be ordered.

Mini-projects are projects that can be wrapped up in a lesson or two. An example of a mini-project might be to show learning visually by making a poster or to turn a reading lesson into a fun reader's theater demonstration. In math, students can use manipulatives or objects to make arrays come to life and then make a display of the three-dimensional arrays for the classroom. In my experience, children love projects, and I love teaching and coaching children individually while they work on projects.

6) **Add manipulatives and "be the teacher" to phonics lessons.** When working on phonics, I usually add magnetic letters, sorting columns (with open or closed word sorts), and sound boxes to lessons. Sometimes, I adapt the phonics and word sorting activities from decoding words to encoding words with each child using a dry-erase marker and a dry-erase board. I give each student a different word to encode on their board, and then they "teach" the word or strategy to the others, blending the phonemes, chunks, onset-rime, or syllables of the word (depending on the lesson). Students love to be the teacher, and they also love to be the students when their peer is the teacher!

All these examples are simple ways to adapt "one-size-fits-all" lessons to the needs of your students. Ready-made curricula can be a foundation to build on for constructivist teachers who then adapt the lessons to increase student engagement and tailor them to where students can construct knowledge based on what they know and what they need to learn.

An Example of Adapting Materials to a Constructivist Approach

In my reading intervention lessons, I sometimes adapt the materials by switching out the books to more engaging texts – books the students (and I) can get excited about! I do this to keep the students' attention if they are reluctant readers. For early and transitional readers, I rely on series books by brilliant authors such as Fran Manuchkin, Nikki Grimes, Dav Pilkey, and Cynthia Rylant. Switching to a trade book series for a short time helps me still teach students where they are while getting more engagement by using texts that we can't put down. I rarely teach with reading passages because they can be tedious, often lack meaning, or are poorly written.

At the beginning of the school year, or when I have students with very little reading stamina, I add in a simple process I call "peanut butter and jelly" reading. I'm not quite sure why this is so popular in my classroom, but the students love it, and it works. You need two copies of a highly engaging text. Partners are assigned to be "peanut butter" or "jelly." Peanut butter always reads first. So, peanut butter reads the first page/section, and jelly reads along silently in their own copy of the text. When peanut butter finishes, jelly asks peanut butter a question central to the story (No yes or no questions.) Peanut butter answers. Jelly determines if peanut butter is correct or if peanut butter should read it again to learn the answer.

Next jelly reads, and peanut butter silently reads along with their eyes. Peanut butter asks the question and determines if jelly understood or should read again. The students are practicing reading fluency, comprehension, word solving, and rereading skills. Their reading stamina grows. I listen in on the reader, and then I listen in on the question and answer.

Sometimes, it happens that the questioner wasn't listening. Then they must ask the reader to reread, which will help them form a question. Forming questions like this is not easy. The children have to come up with an appropriate question that is central to the story and pertains to the page they are on. I love watching this process. But I do more than watch. I listen in, and I coach the reader and questioner, calling them by the names of peanut butter and jelly. Last year, we needed to have a group of three (which works, you just need to have two questioners). We landed on peanut butter, jelly, and pickles. One third grader who was "pickles" decided she'd rather be Nutella.

After a few days of peanut butter and jelly reading, we move back to using a wide variety of texts, with students reading the entire text on their own. After that, in my intervention lessons, PB&J reading becomes a fun activity reserved for special occasions and sometimes the last few days of school.

This is one way constructivist teachers get creative to move students from frustration to engagement. We stay true to the learning goal while getting students to start to lean in, have some success, and enjoy the learning process.

BOX C   Literature Connections for the Classroom

I love to use series books in reading intervention lessons because students often pick up the next book in the series to read independently, eliciting many wonderful chats about books. Here are a few children's book series I like to use for peanut butter and jelly reading:

♦ Bailey School Kids Graphic Novels by Marcia Thornton Jones and Debbie Dadey
♦ Dragon Series by Dav Pilkey
♦ Katie Woo and Pedro Mysteries by Fran Manuchkin
♦ King and Kayla Mysteries Series by Dori Hillestad Butler
♦ Ling and Ting Series by Grace Lin
♦ Miami Jackson Series by Patricia McKissak
♦ Mr. Shivers Series by Max Brallier
♦ Mrs. Wishy Washy Series by Joy Cowley
♦ Nikki and Deja Series by Nikki Grimes
♦ Pickles the Dog Series by Michele Dufresne
♦ Ricky and Buster Series by Katherine Rawson
♦ Sophia Martinez Series by Jacqueline Jules
♦ Spy Busters Series by Ellen Lewis
♦ Who Was/Is? Series by various authors
♦ Who Would Win? Series by Jerry Pallotta

Questions for Adapting Materials to a Constructivist Approach:

♦ How might each of the six ways to adapt curricular materials promote deeper learning?
♦ What are some examples of times that you have adapted curricular materials to fit the students you have?

◆ What are some examples of times you have adapted curricular materials to make the lesson more meaningful and engaging?

REFLECTION BOX D

What questions do you have for

ADAPTING MATERIALS TO A CONSTRUCTIVIST APPROACH?

The Power of Choice (Dana)

Nothing motivates students like choice. The ability to make a choice is deeply embedded in human nature. We all like to make our own choices. Yet, students often spend most of their school day with others deciding for them. When they come home from school, they can't wait to do what they want to do. However, when I talk to teachers about classroom choice, they often panic. I think they think of chaos instead of choice. "Students don't always make good choices," they tell me. But remember, you, the teacher, make all of the selections that will be offered. If there is a poor choice, don't offer it.

The power of choice depends on the students feeling like they are making their own decisions. They need to feel that they are trusted to choose for themselves. Simultaneously, as the teacher, I want accountability for their time. So I use the Planning Cycle (Figure 3.1). Borrowed from the High Scope Foundation many years ago, their Plan, Do, and Review cycle works. It allows children to feel they are making choices about their work and allows the teacher to hold them accountable for their choice time.

I use the Planning Cycle anytime students enter a choice time in the daily schedule, which may include learning centers, recess, or project work. For now, let us focus on learning centers.

Planning Time is when students decide what they will do during Work Time. I like to refer to the activities students choose

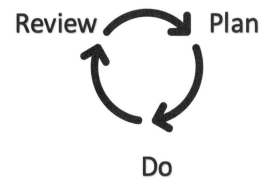

FIGURE 3.1 The Planning Cycle

as their "work." The key to this part of the cycle is to make all the choices clear and create an easy method for selecting the order students will use to make their choices. It must feel fair to them.

A planning board, displayed for everyone to see clearly, tells the students their options and how many people are allowed in that activity or space. When they select an activity, one slot is filled. When all the slots are filled, students will make another choice. That's life.

Part of the power of the Planning Cycle is when students declare what work they are choosing to do out loud. It is a declaration of their plans, and it becomes a commitment. Declaring your commitment to your work aloud to your peers is a powerful lesson for life and a cornerstone of a constructivist education. Children tend to follow through on the commitments they make publicly.

For learning center time, students answer two questions:

♦ What center will I choose?
♦ What work will I do?

For example, when it is their turn, a student may declare, "Today I'm going to the art center, and I'm going to make my mom a birthday card because it's her birthday." Teachers may ask for clarifications, encourage elaboration of a plan, or say, "We'll look forward to seeing what you make at Sharing Time (Review)." But the seed is planted in the student's mind: My work is important; My work is interesting, and my teacher wants to see what

I can do with my work. The planning time should take about 10 minutes. It is whole group and somewhat teacher directed.

Work Time (Do) is when students put their plans into action. With repetition, students get more confident in working on their plans. But plans can change. The dynamics of a group may influence a plan. Plans may evolve as students work collaboratively on one of their ideas. How the plans change or evolve may become the focus of a discussion at Review Time.

Work Time becomes a perfect opportunity to conduct small-group learning sessions. I recommend you spend the first few weeks of the school year establishing procedures for Work Time before you begin small-group time. About 45–60 minutes of center/work time is necessary for students to go deeply into their work. If students have 15 minutes in a teacher-led small group, that leaves about 30–45 minutes to work at centers.

Review Time is the payoff for students. If you have been asked to commit, and you put your plan into action during the Work Time, the Review Time is when students share what they accomplished. It is time for students to talk about their work: to explain, share, and show pride in their work. The cycle breaks down without Review Time.

Review Time is student talk. Students share what they accomplished during Work Time. They may bring their products to share. A group of students who worked together at a learning center may discuss their work as a team. You can take pictures during Work Time to show during Review Time, which helps students see and share what they accomplished. Review Time completes the cycle by asking students to discuss their plans for the next learning center time. About 10 minutes is enough because not every child must share daily, but each child should share one or two times a week. Older students can share in a center time log, writing or drawing their plan at Plan Time and writing or drawing what they did at Review Time. This is an authentic purpose for writing that can be revisited each day.

Regrettably, Review Time can be the easiest to drop when teachers find themselves running out of time and needing to move on in the schedule. But without an opportunity to share one's work, students have learned a less appealing message; there is no need to make any real plans for my work. A successful Review Time makes all the difference in the students' sense of efficacy and in the next day's learning.

Now that we have the Planning Cycle in place, we can focus on learning centers. A learning center is a small-group area in the classroom where students independently explore open-ended tasks. Broad topics work best. For example, art, construction, writing, books, and math manipulatives, games/puzzles are some traditional learning centers. The center space is clearly defined to accommodate a small group of students. Depending on the amount of space and the task you provide, the area may work for two to six students.

Tasks are the open-ended materials you add to the learning center. Begin simply with two to four tasks and add more as the student's work demands a boost to inspire new ideas for work. Here are some ideas for choosing open-ended tasks. Blocks are open-ended. Worksheets are not. Writing for a purpose is open-ended. Practicing writing high-frequency words is not. Making collage art like Eric Carle is open-ended. Making a craft butterfly (as the only choice) is not.

In open-ended tasks, students bring their ideas to the work. Demonstrating their thinking, interests, and creativity, students allow you to see what they can do. Students may work on the same idea for days. They may recruit other students who contribute to the ideas they discussed at Review Time. The work changes and grows as the year goes on. For many children, this is the best part of their day.

Example for the Power of Choice

If you have raised a child, you may know more than you think about the power of choice. At around 2 years old, many children like to pick out their clothes to wear for the day. The problem is they don't always have the logic to do it successfully.

For example, your child may choose their favorite sundress on a snowy winter day. And if you try to explain why they shouldn't wear it, the struggle is on.

At about this stage, parents figure out the power of choice. You help your child feel like they are picking out their clothes by first saying, "I know you want to pick your outfit to wear, so since you're getting so big, I think you should get to pick too." Offer two appropriate choices. Sold correctly, it feels like a choice to your child. This works with drinks and snacks. "Today, you get to pick what you want to drink. You can choose either milk or water." The child feels like they have the power, and that is, after all, what 2-year-olds want.

It works after age 2 as well. A friend told me that when her mother took her and her two sisters shopping for back-to-school clothes with the pledge that they were going to get to pick out their favorites, she would put them each into three of the dressing rooms and tell them: "These little rooms are very hard to get. So, guard yours carefully. And while you are guarding your room, I'll bring you clothes that you can pick from." My friend told me that this strategy worked for years and that she and her sisters would brag to their friends that they were allowed to pick out all their clothes.

The power of choice is undeniable. We all like to make our own choices, and the school day improves when it is infused with choice. Constructivist teachers understand the power of choice and facilitate the process.

Questions for the Power of Choice:

♦ What are some open-ended tasks you could add to your learning centers?

♦ Do you make room in your schedule for the Planning Cycle? What could happen if you did?

♦ Why is it important for children to make a commitment to their own learning?

♦ How can you facilitate choice in your classroom? Are there areas where you can add more appropriate choices for students?

REFLECTION BOX E

What questions do you have for

THE POWER OF CHOICE?

Project Work (Dana)

Project work is another time in your daily schedule that can be designed for student choice. Project work allows for in-depth study of an interesting topic. Social studies and science topics make solid study for project work.

Topics should be broad. Topics may come from the school's curriculum, or they may come from the students themselves. In either case, begin by exploring what students know about the topic. It is a way to warm up the brain around the topic. The goal is to uncover questions your students can use to explore the topic deeply.

Examples of topics for project work include the following:

♦ Human Body
♦ Stars and Planets
♦ Zoo Animals
♦ Farm
♦ Bridges
♦ The City
♦ Garden
♦ Families

Begin with a whole-group discussion about the topic. Write the topic in large letters on chart paper placed where it is clearly visible. Ask the students to share what they know about the topic and record their answers on the chart paper. Accept all answers, even if they do not appear to be related to the topic. Encourage students to relate their connections to the topic. For example, a child may say, "I went to my uncle's farm." You can write on the chart: *Juan's uncle has a farm.* Even record misconceptions.

For example, during a discussion about the zoo, a child might say, "They don't have giraffes at the zoo because they are too tall." Discovering misconceptions and changing our opinions is a vital part of project work.

On the next day, make a second chart filled with our questions about the topic. You may say, "Yesterday we talked about families, and you knew a lot. Today, I am curious about what you want to know about families. What questions do you have about families?" Record their answers and place students' names beside their questions.

Place both charts where they can be referenced often throughout the project. You can point out when something new is learned or a question arises and add it to the charts. Add items to the charts as the project goes along. When you read books, use an expert, or go on a field trip, go back to the charts to record what new questions were revealed or what questions were answered.

> Projects can be designed based on the students' responses to these two questions:
> What do you know about _____?
> What would you like to know about _____?

Design activities that allow students to explore the topic. All the children can do the same activity, or if you design four to six activities per week, you can enable students to select an activity they would like to do, or students may work in small groups. Activities should feel open-ended, such as research work, work on technology, or work with materials in learning centers. Whatever the activity, make the connection to their questions from the charts. Provide each student a place to keep the materials they create so that work may continue for days or even weeks.

An example of activities for a project on the topic "farm":

♦ Find pictures of different types of barns and create them using Legos.
♦ Figure out what type of fencing works best for different animals and make two or three examples using recycled materials showing which animal should go with each fence.

- ♦ Make a diagram that shows the process of making milk, starting with the cow and ending with how it arrives at our school cafeteria.
- ♦ Replicate the farm we visited on our field trip with building blocks.
- ♦ Compare a dairy farm to a farm that grows food for a farmer's market.

Field trips and expert visits add to the richness of learning during project work. Plan and schedule both field trips and expert visits throughout the project, not just as a culminating event. Experts may bring hands-on experiments or examples of their work for students to see and explore. Tools that a gardener uses may seem simple, but they may provide an experience that students have never been able to see and hold before. Add to the chart of questions after each experience.

Read aloud many books on the topic to students throughout the project. Include both fiction and nonfiction books. Students may each keep a journal of their experiences throughout the project. Plan for time during the project wrap-up for writing an entry about what they worked on, what they learned, and what questions they uncovered. Encourage students to draw pictures of their work. Journals are a wonderful way for students to consider what they have learned. It can also serve as the Review Time discussed in the last section.

A project may last a week or easily go longer, depending on questions students are still discovering. Plan each week's activities based on new questions from the previous week.

Example for Project Work

I visited a kindergarten classroom while they were learning about community helpers. This week, the focus was on firefighters. The teacher had invited a local firefighter to visit her classroom and talk to the students about the equipment he used in his work.

The man arrived with a large tub of clothing and equipment. He was dressed casually in shorts and a T-shirt. He placed the tub in front of the students seated on the floor in a large carpet area. He told the students he would get dressed as if he were going on a "call" to extinguish a fire.

Saying very little, the firefighter began to pull out each item from the tub. As he did, he said what the item was. "These are my pants with suspenders attached to them to hold them up because they are very heavy." And then, he put on the pants. He continued with gloves, boots, a helmet, and the various tools he attached to a belt. He was labeling each item and its purpose as he put them on.

The teacher sat beside him at a chart stand, and she recorded each item as he put them on and made a simple drawing of the item beside the label.

The children were mesmerized by this demonstration. After getting fully dressed, he removed each item and allowed the students to touch them, feel the weight, or try them on. They felt how heavy the boots were. They discovered how thick the gloves were. Then, they went to the school's parking lot to explore the fire truck parked there.

After the guest left, the students worked on projects connected to the fire equipment they had learned about. They made a before and after drawing of the firefighter by dividing a sheet of art paper in half, drawing him in his shorts and T-shirt on one half and fully dressed in his equipment on the other. They created suspenders for their pants out of ribbons. They dressed a doll in fire equipment made from art materials and wrote thank you notes, referring to the chart the teacher had created for the words they wanted to incorporate into their letters.

This simple expert visit was rich beyond compare. It allowed the students to see each item without overly explaining. It was not a lecture where the information became lost in too much talk. It was powerful and memorable—the goal of project work.

Questions for Project Work:

♦ What topics are your students interested in learning?
♦ How can you balance both science and social studies topics in project work?

- ♦ What is the value of asking students what questions they have uncovered throughout the project?
- ♦ What types of topics would work better in project work?

REFLECTION BOX F

What questions do you have for

PROJECT WORK?

Assigning vs. Teaching (Krista)

Constructivist teachers employ a "one at time, all at once" approach to classroom instruction where student ownership and engagement in the learning community are foundational. This happens with class meetings, student choice, differentiated learning, and projects.

No more sitting at the desk and handing out the "work." (Then, grading the pile of work that comes back to the desk!) We ensure the students get ample modeling, front-loading, discussion, and practice before releasing students to independence. This makes sure we teach for understanding and monitor student practice before assessing the student's skill level. It decreases confusion created by partial understanding of a concept, possibly because mastery was expected too soon before learning and formative assessment took place.

Constructivist teachers are mindful of this question – are we teaching or assigning? Review this diagram of Regie Routman's Optimal Learning Model (OLM), an explicit depiction of the gradual release model for instruction (Figure 3.2). What do you notice? Which sections of the OLM would be where teaching takes place? How about assigning? And which one has more applications? A high priority for constructivist teachers is choosing effective teaching strategies within a gradual release of responsibility model, such as the OLM.

We can use this OLM to ensure we fully teach concepts through demonstration, modeling and then practice with the

Who Holds Book/Pen	Degree of Explicitness/Support
Teacher/Student	▼ Demonstration
Teacher/Student	▼ Shared Demonstration
gradual handover of responsibility	
Student/Teacher	▼ Guided Practice
Student/Teacher	▼ Independent Practice

Optimal Learning Model Across the Curriculum

DEPENDENCE   **INDEPENDENCE** ➤

Ongoing Assessment & Celebration

To Learners	With Learners		By Learners
I DO IT	**WE DO IT**	**WE DO IT**	**YOU DO IT**
Demonstration	**Shared Demonstration**	**Guided Practice**	**Independent Practice**
teacher	*teacher*	*student*	*student*
• initiates • models • explains • thinks aloud • shows how to "do it"	• demonstrates • leads • negotiates • suggests • supports • explains • responds • acknowledges	• applies learning • takes charge • practices • problem solves • approximates • self-corrects	• initiates • self-monitors • self-directs • applies learning • problem solves • confirms • self-evaluates
student	*student*	*teacher*	*teacher*
• listens • observes • may participate on a limited basis	• listens • interacts • questions • collaborates • responds • tries out • approximates • participates as best he can	• scaffolds • validates • teaches as necessary • evaluates • observes • encourages • clarifies • confirms	• affirms • assists as needed • responds • acknowledges • coaches • evaluates • sets goals
instructional context	*instructional context*	*instructional context*	*instructional context*
• thinking aloud • reading and writing aloud • direct explanation	• shared reading and writing • interactive reading and writing • shared read aloud • scaffolded conversations	• guided reading and writing experiences • partner reading and writing • reciprocal teaching • literature conversations	• independent reading and writing • informal conferences • partner reading and writing • homework and assignments

handover of responsibility

Ongoing Assessment & Celebration

Teaching Essentials by Regie Routman (Heinemann: Portsmouth, NH); © 2008

FIGURE 3.2 The Optimal Learning Model

The Optimal Learning Model is reprinted with permission from Regie Routman, author of *Writing Essentials* (2004) and *Reading Essentials* (2002), published by Heinemann.

students. After that, we hand over the responsibility to the student. We offer guided practice with small groups to help each student right where they need help. Finally, after modeling, shared practice, and guided practice, we release our students to independent practice.

Using this gradual release model when planning instructional units and lessons will help us make sure we thoroughly teach concepts from a meaningful whole. Children need to understand the big picture of what we are teaching. After that, we can address the individual parts and, next, connect the parts back to the meaningful whole, which is the goal of our instruction.

Constructivist teachers want to ensure children have plenty of modeling and demonstration before shared and guided practice. We then informally observe learning during shared and guided practice, taking anecdotal notes. Are the students ready to do this on their own? Or do they need more shared or guided practice? Maybe they need another approach? Possibly more modeling and demonstration? I often experience that students have confusions they need to work through before being able to do something new. It's essential to take the time to address confusions and help the student sort those out. This can take extra time and teaching before they take off in their learning. Some people call this going slow so that we can go fast.

It is important to reiterate that constructivist teachers work whole to part. For example, when writing a personal narrative, some students need to work on using descriptive language to help us clearly understand what happened to them (their personal story). Others need to learn how to work from their prewriting to get their ideas to the page. Still others must focus on letter formation, spelling, or punctuation to make their story readable. The whole is the completed personal narrative. The parts are the skills needed to complete the meaningful whole. Students may need different parts, so a nuanced approach to assignments needs to happen. We can work individually with students on the parts they uniquely need or pull flexible small groups for students who need the same instruction to accomplish the whole. In this way, we are working toward each child getting the next steps in their own learning process.

When we assign learning tasks to students, this is their independent work. As a constructivist teacher, we have a degree of confidence that the students are ready to do the task on their own when assigning independent work. In addition, we are prepared to have a mini-conference to help when needed. However, once we've assigned a learning task, it is with some evidence that the student is ready to do it independently. This moves us away from the more behaviorist "one-size-fits-all" approach of teaching prepared lessons in a prescribed order to the whole group, whether they need them or are ready for them.

Remember that the Optimal Learning Model of instruction is not linear. We move through the experiences based on what children need. Pay particular attention to ensuring each stage of the OLM is considered in every new learning experience. If we give students an independent learning project or assignment and almost every child has questions, we know we've handed over the responsibility too soon. This has happened to me so many times! That's okay. We circle the wagons, get together, and figure out what needs to happen next to prepare students for independence.

It is important to remember that when asking students to work independently, it doesn't mean the teacher is not involved or uses the time to work on something else. As constructivist teachers, we observe and monitor independent work to see what has been learned.

During independent time, we observe and offer feedback, take anecdotal notes, informally assess, and celebrate the learning that is taking place. We might conduct mini-reflection conferences with students, asking them to share their learning. These can be recorded and shared with parents at student-led or teacher-led parent-teacher conferences.

During independent learning time, we also monitor to ensure that the student hasn't misunderstood the assignment and gets off to a rough start. We do this by working the room to spend a minute next to each child as they work or possibly reading over shoulders to check for understanding. This makes it less likely for the teacher to devote significant time to grading and correcting papers at home because some of it can be done while checking in with students.

For example, we can avoid the case of a student getting ten similar math problems wrong on an assignment. The teacher can ask students to raise their hands after the first three to ensure they have the concept. For those who need to correct them, we now know some additional teaching needs to occur before the students are ready for independent demonstration of their understanding. Students can solidify their confusion about the concept by practicing it incorrectly, so doing it badly may be worse than not doing it at all.

I love the quote, "Practice doesn't make perfect; practice makes permanent." This means we must quickly catch a student's misunderstanding before it becomes permanent. For example, with primary children, when students are learning word families or working on high-frequency words independently, we check in often to ensure they are on the right track.

A typical example of this is misspelling words because students may hear the sounds differently and put them in the wrong word family "file folder" in their minds. This can happen with words like "sat" (set) and "saw" (sall), "and" and "in"! The more times a child spells "they" with an "a" rather than an e, the more permanent it becomes. These confusions take time to unlearn.

I picture the gradual release of responsibility stages as having bridges from one stage to the next and back again. We move through the stages as needed, ensuring we build a strong foundation for each child as a learner. This is how students reach higher levels of rigor within their learning. We honor the process as much as the product by teaching more than assigning.

Example for Assigning vs. Teaching

I have heard many high school teachers say they wish students would come to them being able to write a complete sentence. I know middle school teachers who say they wish the students would come to them being able to write a complete sentence. And upper elementary teachers say it too. I get it. Yet I feel the need to testify that I did teach the first graders to write a complete sentence! And I know most of us did the same.

Where is the disconnect here? I think it is in the way we teach grammar and writing. I have the belief that children need to write first. Get their language and ideas on paper. Then edit for sentence structure, punctuation, capitalization, and all the conventions. Whole to part.

Here's an example of how I like to teach this. I love the personal narrative unit. It's when we learn all about writing through telling our own stories. It's not our whole life story, just events where something happened, something changed, and it's a story we want to tell and maybe have told many times. When we tell our own story, we have probably already spoken the words multiple times. We know it by heart. We have already had the words in our language.

I love to demonstrate writing personal narratives with stories that are universal. I don't write about my trip to Yellowstone or my summer vacation when I flew to a beach resort. The students may be unable to relate to that experience and see it in their minds. I demonstrate with something we've all experienced, such as having a loose tooth or the first day of school. With older students, I like to write about how, in fourth grade, a teacher mispronounced my name all year (that happened!) or when I chipped my tooth while riding my bike and ran into a tree (also really happened).

Also, there are many short and fun read-aloud books about losing a tooth. We read some of these books and retell the stories. We talk about the details the author described and how they write a beginning, middle, and end to their story. Then, I write my loose tooth story on a chart paper. First, I tell my story out loud to the students, who are all sitting at my feet. Then, I ask them to partner up and retell my story. Then "we" write it on chart paper. I hold the marker, and the students help me remember. We get it all down. The next day, we revise. And the day after that, we edit. We check to ensure I have a beginning, middle, and ending. (I like to do this on three chart papers – beginning, middle, and end – because it makes it very concrete for students to replicate later.)

After that, we go back to one of the loose tooth books. We read it again. We get in groups of three and retell the story. One person retells the beginning, one the middle, one the end. Then they write their part down. This takes some coaching and scaffolding on my part. I move from group to group. The next day, they revise their parts. And the day after that, they edit. Finally, the next day, the students stand up in their groups with their parts and read them to the class. (Revising and editing become more important to you when you're going to read your writing to the class!) We celebrate.

Now we're ready for independent writing, to tell our own loose tooth story individually, starting by orally sharing our stories in the writing circle. Each child gets their own three pieces of paper. We get to work. Over the week, we'll individually go through the same process. After that, we'll do it all again, but it might be a personal narrative about getting a new baby or new pet in our family. Or maybe about a time we fell on the playground and had to go to the nurse. As a class, we all may need to go back and review what to do, or only some of us do. That's okay; we now have so many examples right here in our classroom that it will be easy to review.

Let's go back to those complete sentences. When we teach whole–part–whole like this, a complete sentence is a means to communicate our story. It matters. Doing this process with the goal of writing a complete sentence might have felt like a mundane, disjointed task – something to do for the teacher. But writing a personal story that must be full of complete sentences is another experience altogether.

Questions for Assigning vs. Teaching:

- ♦ What areas in our curriculum do we often assign more than we teach?
- ♦ What areas in our instruction can we add more "we do" or shared and guided practice?
- ♦ How can we add the OLM to our planning process?
- ♦ Think of times you assigned too soon – what happened? And what actions did you take?

REFLECTION BOX G

What questions do you have for

ASSIGNING VS. TEACHING?

The Heart of Teaching One at a Time, All at Once (Dana)

One at a time, all at once is a glimpse into the daily workings of a constructivist classroom where children work independently, in small groups, and in whole groups. Choice and engagement are the foundation of this work. Choice plus engagement equals ownership, a powerful formula for creating a child-centered classroom experience. With ownership in their learning, and ample opportunities for modeled, shared and guided practice, children are motivated to learn more. It is less about what is supposed to be learned and more about wanting to know.

One fall morning, I stood outside an elementary school waiting to meet with a group of teachers. I had met with them earlier that summer to work on incorporating choice into their practices. As we waited for the doors to open, I overheard a conversation between a small group of students from one of the classrooms where I had been working. One boy was leading a very animated discussion describing what his plans were for their learning center time. He had thought about his plan and knew just what he would do when the time came to choose their learning centers. He said, "Today I'm going to the Lego center, and I'm going to build a front loader that really works. I saw one with my dad, and I know how it works. I'm going to build it myself." Several of his friends picked up on his enthusiasm and asked if they could join him. The boy agreed but added, "Yes, but remember, I'm in charge!" That is the definition of ownership.

How often do students talk about their learning to others outside of school? I recently asked a friend's kindergartener what the best part of her school day is, and she said, "When it's time to go home." What a contrast in experiences! We want children to think about their learning and feel they have ownership. I would suggest that it only happens when a child knows they will be asked about their plans, when they know they have a choice in their learning activities, and when they trust they will be allowed to become fully engaged.

4

Literacy with Heart

Literacy instruction taught from the heart is central to a constructivist teacher's daily practice. This heartbeat of a constructivist classroom, using meaningful literacy instruction, should include many different instructional strategies each day. Yet, it always consists of a passion for teaching literacy authentically while building on each child's reading and writing process right where they are.

Authentic literacy instruction means all children are readers and writers receiving responsive lessons centered on each child's individual learning needs and growth. Each child is allowed to develop their individual reading process through different means. You will unlikely find children identified as low or high and tracked accordingly. This chapter reviews many instructional strategies and daily practices regularly utilized in a constructivist approach to literacy.

Reading Mileage (Krista)

Noted literacy expert Pat Cunningham (2005) wrote about how it's hard to become a better reader when you don't read very much. Yet, we've watched many reading lessons where the students did little to no actual reading. They are practicing the parts of reading, talking about reading, and getting ready to read, but not reading. At some point, I started to address this as

DOI: 10.4324/9781032707921-5

"eyes-on-text" time, meaning the act of reading continuous text across the page minute after minute. When children do that a lot, they are gaining *reading mileage*. The more "miles" a child reads, supports the creation of a disposition for reading, a reading identity or knowing what tastes I have as a reader, and more successful practice.

Constructivist teachers pay particular attention to the students' "eyes-on-text" time because they know the student must build an effective reading process through a great deal of successful independent reading along with challenging reading with prompting and support. Each child *constructs* their individual reading process where phonics, fluency, and comprehension are intertwined into a fluid process where children can engage in more complex texts.

The amount of time students have "eyes on text" is crucial to their reading development. This can be done with many highly effective literacy practices, including the following:

♦ Shared reading or close reading
♦ Small-group reading
♦ Independent reading

Shared Reading

Shared reading is when we all read the same text together – teacher and students. This may be a whole group or a focused small group. The teacher's "big" voice leads while the students' "small" voices follow along in time – or even a step behind. This practice helps students integrate all of the parts of reading and practice in a very supportive environment. Students are free to make mistakes as the chorus moves along. While reading, they practice and learn, practice and learn. When a student hears the text in their ears while reading it out loud and following along with their eyes, the reading process deepens for each child.

Scarborough's Reading Rope (2001), illustrated in Figure 4.1, depicts the many brain activities the reader applies at once while reading. The top thread of the reading rope represents the *meaning* aspect of reading, including background knowledge, vocabulary, language structures, verbal reasoning, and literacy

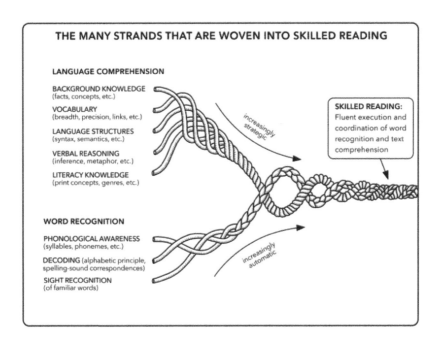

FIGURE 4.1 Scarborough's Reading Rope

Scarborough, H. S. (2001). Connecting early language and literacy to later reading (dis) abilities: Evidence, theory, and practice. In S. Neuman & D. Dickinson (Eds.), *Handbook for research in early literacy* (pp. 97–110). New York: Guilford Press. Reprinted with permission of Guilford Press.

knowledge. The equally important lower thread of the reading rope represents the *print* aspects of reading, including phonological awareness, decoding, and sight recognition. Each strand is loosely connected in the beginning as the "parts" of reading just mentioned are developing.

Print, or word recognition, skills increase in their automaticity as time goes on. Meaning, or language comprehension skills, increases in strategic action as time goes on. In Dr. Scarborough's original drawing, she had a time continuum drawn across the bottom of the graphic, showing that the process of reading develops over time. The strands of the rope become tighter as the reader becomes skilled in bringing print and meaning together into one tightly woven reading process. This process happens within each child's individual time frame. When we look at the many components of reading where the threads are intertwined, tightly woven, and working simultaneously, it seems obvious that one would need a great deal of successful practice weaving all of these skills together and using them simultaneously as a reader!

Close reading is powerful for struggling readers who often do not have the opportunity to master a text. Close reading differs from shared reading in that the text is usually read three times with three different purposes for reading. Sometimes, an excerpt of a longer text is reread closely with a particular eye for vocabulary, figurative language, fluency, phrasing, or another reading goal that can be mastered through repeated readings rather than constantly encountering new texts. Close reading is also powerful for skilled readers to increase their reading skills across various text genres.

Shared and close reading, when practiced daily for about 10 to 20 minutes, is foundational to small-group reading, where the student does the reading on their own with the teacher's coaching and support. Daily shared reading "lifts up" the small-group reading lesson by practicing the same reading strategies and skills together that will be utilized individually in the small-group lesson.

Small-Group Reading

A small-group reading lesson takes an average of 20 minutes, with about half of the time spent in the act of reading texts in the child's zone of proximal development. Many of these reading lessons begin with a second reading or a familiar reading of the text from the previous lesson. Then the teacher provides a rich introduction and orientation to a new text. Next, students read quietly or silently while the teacher listens in and coaches one reader.

The teacher's coaching supports the student's use of strategic action within all of Scarborough's Reading Rope components wherever the child demonstrates needed support. After that, the teacher facilitates a rich conversation about the text, nudging the students' abilities to retell, infer, analyze characters, use nonfiction text features, or other aspects of reading comprehension. Finally, toward the end of the lesson, the teacher picks a quick teaching point to offer to all students within the just-read text. This teaching point is derived on the spot from the readers' needs, the text, and grade-level curriculum options for a focal point of the conversation.

The small-group reading lesson ends with a few minutes of word work that can be applied to reading the next day's text. This applied phonics is an effective way to teach for transfer from whole- and small-group phonics lessons to reading connected texts in small-group reading or writing lessons. As phonics expert Wiley Blevins (2019) states, "Students progress at a much faster rate in phonics when the bulk of instructional time is spent on applying the skills to authentic reading and writing experiences, rather than isolated skill-and-drill work" (p. 6). Blevins advises that at least half of phonics instruction should be teaching for transfer to using phonics in connected texts.

In small-group guided reading, new texts are introduced daily, and the students often add the "old" books to a book bag and reread the texts in a partner reading workstation they attend when not with the teacher at the reading table. As you can see, a lot of "eyes on text" happens in a typical small-group reading lesson. One small-group reading lesson probably won't change a student's life, but three times a week over the school year – approximately 120 lessons – now that can make a huge difference for a reader!

Independent Daily Reading

Independent reading is a 20–30 minute time of the instructional day where children choose their texts with the teacher's guidance. This time often begins with a minilesson on a reading skill/ strategy the class can individually apply to their reading. Then, the children read their own texts. The last 5 minutes include a time to write a response in a reading log or a whole-class, circle-time sharing.

I've noticed that independent reading often gets cut from the daily schedule because teachers feel there are too many mandates to "fit in." Independent reading can be seen as a luxury not often mandated. Independent reading is necessary for a successful reading program because it integrates all of the literacy skills, strategies, and lessons we've taught into engaged practice, cementing the child's reading process as a disposition. The neural networks in the brain are set deeper, which develops confidence in readers. Each child's reading identity is born and nurtured. They see themselves as readers who know what they like to read, their favorite authors and favorite books, and have books "on deck" for what they want to read next. The reading mileage increases.

A Note about Writing and Eyes-on-Text Time

When students are encoding, or writing, it is "eyes-on-text" time too. This is very powerful because students are writing their own text. I am talking about when students put their own language on the page from start to finish. This writing often occurs with coaching and support from the teacher, but the child owns the pen. Not filling in the blank, completing the sentence stem, or copying – there may be a place for these practices at times, but they don't count for "eyes-on-text" time. Composing, using all of their phonics, language, and writing skills at once, increases writing experience, which increases writing proficiency.

Just as a runner must log the miles to grow their running muscle, the number of "miles" of reading each child has logged each school year is critical to their development. We believe reading mileage matters. For struggling readers, it matters even more.

BOX A   Literature Connections for the Classroom

Every child should experience these imaginative books depicting the many ways we become readers.

How to Read a Book
by Kwame Alexander and Melissa Sweet
This creative book feels like a sensory poem about the many ways we experience being a reader.

Lola Loves Stories
by Anna McQuinn and Rosalind Beardshaw
The sequel to Lola Loves the Library *in which mom takes Lola to the library. Lola's dad takes Lola to the library on Saturdays. After reading a book each night, Lola acts out the stories the next day.*

> *Miss Brooks Loves Books (and I Don't)*
> by Barbara Bottner and Michael Emberley
> *Miss Brooks, who dresses up for reading circle, goes to great lengths to finally find an appealing book for cynical, funny, and wart-loving Missy.*
>
> *Wild About Books*
> by Judy Sierra and Marc Brown
> *Molly, a librarian, drives the bookmobile into the zoo by mistake. She delights the animals with books and finds the perfect book for each one.*
>
> *My Very Favorite Book in the Whole Wide World*
> by Malcolm Mitchell and Michael Robertson
> *Henley is a great kid who hates to read. He shares how reading is hard for him. One day, Henley gets the scariest assignment in the world – to share your favorite book.*

Example for Reading Mileage

As a literacy specialist who conducts literacy intervention lessons every day for groups of students determined to be struggling readers, there is one conversation I have with the children's classroom teachers over and over. Here is how the conversation usually goes:

Me: *(Insert student's name) is really growing in his reading right now. I'd love to hear what you've been noticing in the classroom.*

Classroom Teacher: *Well, I've noticed his confidence is much better. That makes him try harder in reading.*

Me: *Yes, when students have a lot of successful reading practice, their confidence does improve. I am excited to hear that.*

Classroom Teacher: *I'm glad he finally has some confidence. Before, he wouldn't even try!*

Me: *Yes, I think the confidence results from (student's name) cementing a more solid reading process*

> *while gradually tackling more complex texts. Also,*
> *now that he is reading more from his book bag, he's*
> *getting more skilled as a reader.*
> *Classroom Teacher: Thanks so much for helping with his confidence.*

We often think that students who gain confidence in general then become better readers. However, as this conversation illustrates, it is with effective literacy instruction and successful practice and reading mileage that students gain confidence. Since success begets success, the reader grows and grows. I see this happen in school every day.

Reading mileage is an often overlooked part of effective literacy teaching. It builds confidence. Successful practice at whatever we are learning to do builds confidence. Think tennis, robotics, knitting, anything!!! And, of course, something as complex and inherent to our culture as literacy will require a lot of successful practice.

Questions for Reading Mileage:

- ♦ What is something you are good at? How did you become good at it?
- ♦ When are my students "eyes-on-text" times during each school day?
- ♦ How do I organize time for my students to experience reading mileage?
- ♦ How can I address the reading mileage needs of my students?
- ♦ What can we learn about how children develop a reading process from Scarborough's Reading Rope?

REFLECTION BOX B

What questions do you have for

READING MILEAGE?

Conversations (Not Quizzes) about Books (Krista)

As a young child, I was an avid reader, but my grade in reading was usually no better than average. Why? I think because I hated answering the ten questions at the end of the book. I loved reading the books, discussing the books, and going to the school and public libraries on my own. I didn't mind reading what the teacher wanted me to read. I just really hated answering those questions, and I gave it little effort. In elementary school, my son (a chip off the old block, I guess) was asked to join a reading program where students read books and answer online quizzes after reading the books. The harder the book, the more points you received. He figured out that if he read about half of the book, he could answer most of the questions and get the points required. All the while, he was reading books of his own choice from cover to cover. I think a lot of children feel that way. We need to find ways to make reading comprehension of a book more meaningful and even celebratory of the author, the theme, purpose, and real-life takeaways.

Dana and I believe that our classroom conversations reflect the quality of our teaching. Long gone are the days of quiet classrooms and children being seen and not heard. Children LOVE to talk! And they love to talk about books. When we engage students in talking about texts, we are building their vocabulary, comprehension, and reading proficiency all at once. We also build community, learn about our world, show how we value one another, and discover more about each child's literacy strengths and needs. Constructivist teachers build discussion and dialogue into all aspects of the learning day, especially literacy lessons.

Circle Conversations

I love it when children sit in a circle so we can all easily see each other. It's not a teacher-student, teacher-student, teacher-student conversation. Like on a basketball team, the teacher is the coach; the students are the players; the coach throws the ball to a player; the player always throws the ball back to the coach. Then the coach throws it to the next player. If the player always throws the ball back to the coach, they are not interacting with their teammates. When this happens in the classroom, the conversation can be more artificial, and the children often try to decide what the teacher wants them to say. Our goal is for the ball (conversation) to go around the room with the children listening and adding to each other's comments while looking at each other.

When the "ball" starts getting passed around to each other, a more authentic conversation can happen, and it's more engaging for the students. I find that when more learning and interaction occur, they lean in, and because they like to talk to each other, children tend to be more engaged in the read aloud because they know they'll have the circle conversation with their classmates. This circle conversation fits a constructivist theory because the children construct language on a topic and use their new language and vocabulary in a natural conversation.

We can use a lot of conversation structures to get ALL students talking rather than just the students with their hands up or the students whose popsicle stick is drawn from a cup. Here are some of our favorites:

Turn and Talk: Each child has a talking partner where, at the teacher's signal, they turn knee-to-knee, elbow-to-elbow, and take turns speaking on the topic at hand. I've recently heard this called "Turn and Learn." Students would then report what they learned from their partner. Powerful.

'Round the Circle: Each child takes turns talking on a topic around the circle. In this way, each child's voice has equal time and merit, and the teacher can gauge the child's understanding. 'Round the Circle can be used with various topics or just one, depending on the depth of the subject and the teacher's goals. For example, it's fun to get to the end of a book with a surprise ending, stop and quickly go around the circle to ask students to predict what will happen. Then read the surprise ending. Then go around the circle the other way to react to what actually happened.

Team Talk: Have classroom teams (possible clusters of students at tables or desks) of three or four students with generic designations (such as colors or numbers). For text discussion in the circle, have the Green Team stand up. "Let's listen to the Green Team today." Then invite comments on the Green Team's thinking. Rotate the teams equally and often.

Accountable Talk: Every first-grade teacher has had the experience of asking children a question about a text and having them tell you a prediction, even though you didn't ask children to predict what will happen. This happens over and over again. And not just in first grade. Children of all ages can learn to actively listen to teachers' open-ended questions, which get students to engage and comprehend text more deeply. The teachers can practice redirecting students' conversation to the topic at hand. We do not let them say anything and move on to the next child, which promotes disengagement in lessons. So, in this spirit, accountable talk can be beneficial. Teach children a set of sentence stems to help them get to the type of thinking and conversation we are asking for.

Here are some examples. Every classroom may need different ones. You may want to take it off the list when students are good at one or another, for example, such as "I predict…"

I think…
I predict…
I wonder…
I like…
I question…
I agree with _____ because …
I disagree (or I see it differently)…
I noticed…
I am surprised…
At the beginning…
In the middle…
At the end…
I think the author…

The Power of the Second Question
When we ask a follow-up question after students share their understanding, we can "nudge" them to deeper levels of understanding and skill. We can help them build their vocabulary and

depth of knowledge, all with a second question. Use them often. Help students answer second questions by constructing the language together and then asking the students to share. We can do this by offering some of the words or phrases and letting them finish or by "pulling" some new language out and then helping the students into a complete thought that they can repeat. Asking the second question is a powerful constructivist teaching strategy where students are met where they are and nudged forward in their language and learning.

Dana and I have observed instruction in hundreds of classrooms. Those classrooms where there is "working noise" with children having focused discussions, where children feel comfortable in the back and forth of sharing ideas, and where students come to the circle with ease and purpose and a little gleam of knowing their ideas are valued are some of the landmarks of a constructivist classroom.

Example for Conversations (Not Quizzes) about Books

Dana was talking about her book club the other day and noticed that how we structure authentic book clubs in the classroom is similar to how her book club operates.

She explained that her book club was a group of about 10 to 12 women in her neighborhood who met monthly to discuss a book they had selected to read. They gathered each year in September for the first meeting to choose books. Each person would bring one or two of their favorites they had read over the summer months and "sell" the books to the others.

The process of "selling" the book was interesting because the women would tell just enough about the book to pique interest. Over time, it was clear each member had different genres and authors they favored. The difficult part came when it was time to select one book for each month that would be read. The discussions were lively as each tried to lobby for their favorites.

Once the books were chosen, the group met each month to discuss the books they had read on their own. Those conversations were precisely what children can do as well. They require listening to each other, formulating a response, and thinking about their position. I may love a character, but I discover others found the person unappealing, deceitful, or difficult to understand. Now, I must think whether I also see some of those characteristics or stand by my original position. A lively debate is a hallmark of a constructivist theory. I may have loved my book, but I am surprised others didn't like it very much. We want to hear our students have this type of spirited debate over books!

How could you organize book clubs? How would you structure them? Here are some things you may wish to consider:

♦ How will you help students prepare to "sell" their books?
♦ Would a chart with some suggestions for leading a book club discussion be helpful? Guidelines may include selecting a favorite book, writing two or three points about why they love it, and rereading it to see what else they wish to include in the sales pitch.
♦ How long should a book club last?
♦ As the teacher, what will your role be?
♦ What discussion questions will you use to start the book club conversation? Brainstorm some of the discussion questions with your group.

Book clubs would look different for each grade level. Still, from our younger to our oldest students, book clubs could be an exciting addition to your literacy curriculum.

Questions for Conversations (Not Quizzes) about Books:

♦ How does an in-depth conversation about books deepen your understanding as an adult? What is the correlation to our work with students?
♦ What do you notice about the students' participation in classroom discussions?
♦ How could you structure a book conversation where the "ball" is passed around to engage all and deepen their understanding?
♦ What other structures might you use to get everyone's talk on texts?

REFLECTION BOX C

What questions do you have for

CONVERSATIONS (NOT QUIZZES) ABOUT BOOKS?

Multiple Read Alouds (Krista)

We recommend reading to children more than once a day. Four to seven read alouds is our goal. Our brains remember a story. We learn language through story. Our vocabulary builds from reading stories. The power of demonstrating reading skills, strategies, and "being a reader" cannot be underestimated for all young learners. And, of course, reading mileage. When a book is known through the read aloud, students are more likely to pick it up and read it on their own.

We're not necessarily talking about each of these read aloud experiences being the 20-minute interactive read aloud built into many curricula. Those would ideally be once per day. We are discussing and reading books with children throughout the school day.

Most importantly, if you feel that children did not get all the early years of "lap time" reading they needed to be ready for school, four to seven read aluds a day can supply those experiences once children come to school. We can make a difference for children who come to school not yet ready to learn by upping our read-aloud game. By incorporating whole-class, small-group, and one-on-one lessons with rhyming books such as favorites *I Can Read with My Eyes Shut* by Dr. Seuss, *Hush! A Thai Lullaby* by Mingfong Ho, *I Can't Said the Ant* by Polly Cameron, and *The Gruffalo* by Julia Donaldson, we offer the experience of "lap time" reading. In her book for parents, *Reading Magic*, the illustrious children's book author *and* literacy expert Mem Fox (2001) discusses lap time reading as when there is a shared text, a shared story time experience, and a shared conversation about the book being read aloud.

SUBJECT	TEXT	TEACH	CONNECT
CLASS MEETING 5 MINUTES	*Horsefly and Honeybee* by Randy Cecil	Discuss how the horsefly and honeybee solved their problem.	Brainstorm how we can solve problems by working together.
SCIENCE LESSON 5-10 MINUTES	*Up in the Garden and Down in the Dirt* by Kate Messner	Discuss the elements of nature highlighted in the story.	Contrast what happens above ground and below ground when plants grow.
INTERACTIVE READ ALOUD 20 MINUTES	*Little Red Riding Hood* by Jerry Pinkney	During reading, analyze characters and their actions.	After reading, compare this version to other versions we have read of this popular fairy tale.
WRITING MINI-LESSON 10 MINUTES	*We're Going on a Lion Hunt* by David Axtell	Notice how the events happen in sequence.	Use interactive writing to paraphrase the sequence of events on chart paper.
PHONICS - PHONOLOGICAL AWARENESS 5 MINUTES	*The Rhyming Rabbit* by Julia Donaldson	Read one or two pages of rhymes and recognize the rhyming words.	Link hearing these rhymes to the phonological awareness activities that follow.
CHAPTER BOOK 5 MINUTES	*Yasmin The Superhero* by Saadia Faruqi	Read chapter one and discuss the main character, Yasmin.	Preview the first page of chapter 2. Discuss what children think Yasmin may do next.
MATH LESSON 5 MINUTES	*Two of Everything* by Lily Toy Hong	Read and discuss what is happening in the context of number sense.	Practice skip counting together and continue with math lesson.

FIGURE 4.2 Example of Multiple Read Alouds across the School Day

The four to seven read-aloud books can be shared for many different purposes across the school day. For example, we may be teaching children to read dialogue with expression. And we do that in our interactive read-aloud time. The next read aloud may be based on a math concept we use to start our math lesson. Another read aloud might be at our classroom meeting, where we read a story and discuss the behaviors we want to exhibit in the classroom. Have an awkward ten minutes between lunch and specials? Read a short chapter of a book series you'd love for students to pick up independently later.

Another daily read aloud may be during science or social studies. For example, use Gail Gibbons's *Alligators and Crocodiles* or Jim Arnosky's *Thunderbirds: Nature's Flying Predators* for life science. These authentic texts bring the topic to life. Gibbons and Arnosky write and illustrate gorgeous nonfiction texts for many science topics.

For social studies and literature, we can study Kadir Nelson's majestic illustrations in books such as *Nelson Mandela, Moses,* and *Mama Miti* for a biography unit of study. Make history relevant and interesting by reading historical fiction legends such as *Train to Somewhere* by Eve Bunting, *Grandfather's Journey* by Allen Say, *Ruth and the Green Box* by Calvin Alexander Ramsey or *Encounter* by Jane Yolen. Teach math concepts with engaging classics such as *Amanda Bean's Amazing Dream* by Cindy Neuschwander, *The Lion's Share* by Matthew McElligott, and *One Is a Snail, Ten Is a Crab* by April Pulley Sayre and Jeff Sayre.

Use great examples of various aspects of writing as mentor texts for children's writing development. One of my favorites is *When I Was Five* by Arthur Howard, which has a lovely pattern young writers can mimic. I also love reading *Peter's Chair* by Ezra Jack Keats to teach personal narrative and *Roller Coaster* by Marla Frazee to teach sequencing a story. Reading *Do Like Kyla* by Angela Williams helps children understand the use of repetitive language when writing a story.

In our read alouds, we can study authors, illustrators, themes, and genres based on what we want children to learn. When we read multiple books to demonstrate aspects of writing, children are able to use these techniques in their own writing. For example, if you read many of the Froggy books by Jonathan London, children are better able to pick up the writing style, use of beginning, middle, and end or mimic the time in each book when someone yells "FROGGGGGGGGGGGY!" Or, to develop characters, we can read all of Ezra Jack Keats's books about Peter. Peter is the main character in each book, and students can practice writing stories with a main character after analyzing these texts. I have found that reading a few Q&A books can help students write their own more easily. See Figure 4.2 for an example of a day of read alouds crossing the curriculum.

In one of my reading intervention groups, I have introduced the *Zapato Power!* series about Freddie Ramos, a child superhero with super-powered shoes. These engaging books have turned quite a few of my students into avid readers. Sometimes, I read the first few chapters aloud, chapter by chapter, encouraging children to read the rest of them on their own. We can't assume children know how to read a chapter book. We must demonstrate how, chapter by chapter, the story unfolds and how chapter book writers always leave us hanging at the end of the chapter to entice us to the next chapter, where the author pushes the story forward.

In class meetings, we might dive into character lessons. So we choose books such as *The Very Busy Spider* by Eric Carle, *I Walk with Vanessa* by Kerascoët, or *Your Name is a Song* by Jamilah Thompkins-Bigelow, which can help the class learn about perseverance, kindness, and honoring every child's beautiful name.

Sometimes, we read a quick book or chapter of a series we want children to pick up. Books such as one of the *Elephant and Piggy* books by Mo Willems, a *Ling and Ting* book by Grace Lin, a *Dyamonde Daniel* book by Nikki Grimes, or a *Clubhouse Mysteries* book by Sharon Draper are great when I want some students to get excited about a series. Once I've "blessed" a book this way, I see students add more books they *can* read to their book boxes.

Often, I don't see these "blessed" books again for a long time because they are making the rounds from book box to book box. Children choose those books over and over again, and they know they like them, know who the characters are, and they feel like best friends. Lester Laminack (2016), best friend of the read aloud and literacy expert, describes how books read often can feel like best friends. These classroom favorites are read and reread, and this rereading is fun and excellent for developing fluency, comprehension, and accuracy in reading.

Read alouds are much more than picking up a book and reading it. Some read alouds are quick and take 5 minutes with a small amount of preparation, and some are an event. All are purposely chosen and prepared for the children in front of us. When we know our curriculum *and* our students, we can plan engaging read-aloud experiences where children can meet the text where they are.

This is constructivist literacy learning. As the teacher, I can formulate a shared text experience where one child may improve their short-term memory for retelling a text's beginning, middle, and end. Another child may analyze how the character changes, and I may ask another child to predict what will happen next. I can meet them where they are in their own unique reading development.

When I plan one of those read alouds I called an *event*, I like to think about planning for *before*, *during*, and *after* the read aloud. Planning before the reading hooks students into the book. I love to make connections to other books we've loved and preview the genre and text to get the children ready for the comprehension demands of the text. This means I ask the students to look and listen for specific things. This helps meet instructional goals while also enjoying the book and checking in on students where they are individually. Then I don't have to stop much during the reading, just at critical moments where a discussion is helpful.

After reading, I love to have a circle conversation about the book, where we respond to the different aspects of the text. Sometimes, this includes developing an anchor chart of our collective fundamental understanding of the book we've just spent valuable time reading. But I work not to belabor the books. I choose the teaching points, we read and discuss the book, and move on, knowing that we'll do it all again soon.

Fun Books

Never underestimate the power of a funny book. I have a set of books that I call Friday afternoon books because, honestly, I think I could show up in any classroom on Friday afternoon when it gets a little unruly and mesmerize the children with the text. Most of my Friday afternoon books are funny, some full of suspense, some larger than life.

One example is *John Henry* by Ezra Jack Keats. Once, I used this book with an unruly Boy Scout group my son attended, and the Boy Scout leader was amazed that all of those little boys were leaned in and hanging on every word. Another Friday afternoon book is *My Teacher Is a MONSTER* by Peter Brown. Just the title makes students lean in. *I Wanna Iguana* by Karen Kaufman Orloff is a classic, hilarious book about how a little boy writes notes to his mother, including her terse notes back to the boy. There is also a sequel, *I Wanna New Room*, when a baby brother comes into the picture and the letters go back and forth – equally engaging and delightful.

I adore the *Mercy Watson* series by Kate DiCamillo, about a couple with a pig for a pet and all of the antics that go on with the neighbors and the local pet control. I consider the *Mr. Shivers* series of scary short stories by Max Brallier to be somewhat terrifying myself. These short chapter books are well-written with no blood, gore, or violence and are appropriate for young children, but they will probably still want to check under their beds when they go home.

Over the years, I have witnessed droves of students fall in love with the *Ricky Ricotta* series by Dav Pilkey. I consider these a Friday afternoon book with almost any grade level. I enjoy reading them too. I have an unruly group of third graders in reading intervention at the end of the day right now, so I introduced this series, and they are hooked. I gladly take the last few minutes of each session to read a chapter together. What books do you use to get the students leaned in? I would love to know.

BOX D   Literature Connections for the Classroom

More "Friday afternoon" books I love to read aloud:

Actual Size
by Steve Jenkins
Mesmerizing book of big and small animals and their parts illustrated in their actual size.

What If You Had Animal Teeth?
by Sandra Markle
Learn about animals and their survival by "trying on" their physical features.

I Want My Hat Back
by Mac Barnett
Bear's hat is gone. No one has seen it. What will he do?

Creepy Carrots
by Peter Brown
Jasper Rabbit loves carrots, especially the ones at Crackenhopper Field, until they start to follow him. Everywhere.

It's Only Stanley
by Jon Agee
The Wimbledon's dog, Stanley, is waking the family up at night with the noise he is making in the basement. Each time they decide not to worry because "it's only Stanley." But what is Stanley up to?

Snowmen at Night
by Caralyn Buehner
Have you ever built a snowman only to have it look different the next day? How does this happen? Discover what snowmen might be doing overnight.

After the Fall
by Dan Santat
What happened after Humpty Dumpty had his great fall? He learned how to pick himself up, emotionally put himself back together, and persevere, of course.

Multiple Reads of the Same Book Over a Few Days

I wouldn't read every read aloud multiple times, but I would often have a multiple read aloud going – one book that we read more than once, maybe three or four or five times. With each concurrent reading, I take a different angle or go deeper each time. Or I teach a different concept or learning goal. Every time we reread a book, we also show children the powerful strategy of rereading that we use when we want to understand deeper or when our reading has broken down. All proficient readers do this without exception. For struggling or dyslexic readers, rereading is a crucial strategy. Many of my students in reading intervention lessons depend on those rereads to sort out confusions, comprehend more deeply, and solidify their effective reading process.

Example for Multiple Read Alouds

Let's say we set a goal for an average of five read alouds a day for the school year. That's five read alouds multiplied by 175 days of school, which equals 875 read-aloud experiences and conversations for each child in the classroom. That is a lot of books under the belts of each child in the class (or in the literary experiences section of the brain).

But what if we don't embrace the power of multiple read alouds and read an average of one read aloud each day of the school year? That's 175 read-aloud experiences. That's a big difference in literacy experiences. What do you think will the cumulative effects on students be in the former situation? The latter?

Questions for Multiple Read Alouds:

- ♦ What happens when students experience multiple read alouds each day?
- ♦ When do I read aloud to children? What types of books do I typically read?
- ♦ Where could I add read alouds to my learning day?
- ♦ What might happen for children if I add more repeated read alouds to my day?

REFLECTION BOX E

What questions do you have for

MULTIPLE READ ALOUDS?

Love to Read? (Krista)

Think of something you dislike doing but you have to do a lot. Ugh. How does that feel? You may give it partial attention or rush through, getting it done as quickly as possible. Maybe you avoid it until someone makes you do it.

Now think of something you love to do that you do a lot! Yay. How does that feel? Time flies. You get better and better at it quickly. You allow yourself to make mistakes because you are enjoying yourself and are more likely to take risks when you're having fun and doing something you love.

Reading is like that. When children despise reading, it is harder to help them develop an effective reading process. Our work is easier when children love to read. How can you tell if a child loves to read? Some scream it from the mountaintop I LOVE READING!, but most don't say that. What happens is that they know authors they love and read everything by that author. Others love a series or a particular character.

Some children like to read and be read to but don't believe they are good at it. They may wonder if there is a secret code you need to join the reading club, but no one shared it with them. Developing a reading process can be a rocky road for some children. But we know they have to keep reading. So it is important to remember that children don't have to love to read. Yet, for them to develop as readers, they will progress more smoothly if they love something that they can read about! Maybe they love reading because they love being with their teacher or possibly because they love the camaraderie of shared texts, where they can be seen and heard and a part of the class community. Perhaps there is a topic they love that gets them into books because of the topic they are reading about, such as cooking, rainforest, engines, South Africa, you get the idea.

Do you have beloved children's books and authors? Often, when we love a book, author, or topic, our children will too. We model how to have a reading identity. A reading identity is knowing ourselves as a reader, knowing what we like and don't like. We must use authentic literature in our reading lessons, more literature written by authors and less by content writers who develop materials for publishing companies.

Over and over, I have seen the magical ability of a prolific writer and illustrator to draw the students into the book when a teacher is reading. The pages almost turn themselves. I have also noticed that those books read by or with the teacher often disappear from the display where they sat until the teacher picked them up. Now it's a best friend book, as mentioned earlier. It makes its rounds through the children, one at a time, and ends up in the beloved "best friend book" bin.

My most recent book like that was *Love That Dog* by Sharon Creech. That book opened a world of possibility in my young third-grade readers and disappeared from my display for a long time. Luckily, I saw it pop up in my students' hands and book boxes and at the lunch table – letting me know that it was beloved by many. What an excellent jumping-off point to the rest of Sharon Creech's wonderful collection of books, which I quickly checked out at the library and offered for independent reading.

Example for Love to Read?

I have a student named Sabrina who, in second grade, hated to come to reading intervention group. She seemed to hate me, too, actually. I think Sabrina didn't like being in the group because it made her feel different, singled out, or on display. Sabrina is not diagnosed with dyslexia, but I often wonder what she sees on the page as I listen to her read. As I observe Sabrina's reading, I notice that the more errors she makes, the more she fidgets and guesses at words. Her guesses get less comprehensible as she goes, and she then forgets what the story is even about. And the more she struggles, the more she resists my prompting and support. Our first month together was difficult, and I struggled to find ways to engage Sabrina and support her reading process.

My school district has a district parade every year before Homecoming. I signed up to walk in the parade with my school. It's about two miles of walking, throwing candy along the way, with people lining the streets to yell, dance, and compete to catch the candy. I noticed that Sabrina was there with her grandmother and brother. I was curious if Sabrina would want to talk with me outside of school.

Here's what happened: To my surprise, Sabrina said hello, and then she helped me get my bucket of candy prepared. I was pleased to get to interact with her outside of school. To my surprise, she never left my side for the entire 2 miles and afterward until I got in my car to go. I kept offering her candy, and she refused – saying the candy was for the children (she's a second grader). I realized Sabrina was so self-conscious in reading class that she didn't know I liked her. I realized how much she liked me and wanted to be seen with me. Not because she enjoyed reading but because she apparently liked me. So sometimes children don't love to read, but we can find what they do love and work from that vantage point. And frequently, what they do love is you – their teacher. I can remember feeling the same way about a few of my teachers.

Interestingly, I've taught Sabrina for over a year, and she's made great strides in reading. She still has some hard days, but because we had that Homecoming parade time together, she relaxes into her reading better. She also listens to my prompting because she knows I like her, and she is starting to trust me.

It's great when students love to read, but the truth is that a lot of struggling readers don't love to read. But they love something. Maybe it's superheroes or tigers, trucks, bees, disasters, adventure, travel, or teen life. It's our work to find out what they love and then connect that to their reading lives.

You don't need to change your curriculum. I have another student, Devon, who loves magic and creating paper sculptures and dislikes reading and school in general. At the end of his lesson, I read Brian Selznik's *The Houdini Box* to him for 5 minutes or so. Those 5 minutes tickled his imagination just enough that he would work with me on the necessary phonics and fluency work of the reading lesson first, and then we would read *The Houdini Box* for a few minutes at the end.

Matching books to readers and knowing students' reading identities is integral to a constructivist classroom. Helping students construct a reading identity of their own and nurturing that reading identity and reading life with choice helps them become readers who know what they like to read and what is less attractive. And maybe they will even start to love reading.

Questions for Love to Read?:

◆ Do you love reading? If so, where did the love come from? How has it been sustained?

◆ What children in your classroom don't like to read? Why is this the case?

◆ What could you do to connect something else they love to reading?

◆ What books would you consider Friday afternoon books?

REFLECTION BOX F

What questions do you have for

LOVE TO READ?

Teaching Phonics (Krista)

The purpose of reading is to *construct* the meaning of the text using language and print. Our students must understand that the purpose of printed language is to convey a meaningful message. Therefore, literacy development does include a focus on students' understanding of phonics and phonemic awareness. As constructivist teachers, we intend for our instruction to result in children comfortably using their phonics knowledge while reading connected text for meaning.

Explicit, systematic phonics, spelling, and word work are elements of every classroom day. For younger learners, the general focus is on letter identification, knowledge of letter sounds, individual phonemes, onset and rime, syllables, and patterns in words. For older learners, this knowledge is generally applied to understanding more complex spelling patterns, reading multisyllabic words, and understanding root words, prefixes, and suffixes.

Alphabetic Knowledge

Gone are the days of teaching a letter a week. We use alphabet analogy charts to teach the letters and their analogy (A-apple, B-bear) all at once. We use name charts with each student's name in alphabetical order ("Whose name starts with "S"? Whose name ends with S?" Does anyone have an S in the middle of their name?") and name puzzles to orient children to all of the letters. Using names makes learning personal, and we know that when learning is personal, it is more likely to be internalized.

Once students have learned the letter and name chart, the next step is to assess what letters and sounds the children have learned. Each child will have a different set of known, partially known, and unknown letters and sounds, and we teach from there based on what each child needs.

Children need ample reading and writing activities to practice their understanding of letters and sounds, phonemes, onset and rime, and their first high-frequency words. Reading lots and lots of books makes these isolated phonics skills come to life. I love using alphabet books, fun decodable books, and "learn to read" favorites, such as *Z Is for Moose* by Kelly Bingham, *Who Stole the Cookie from the Cookie Jar* by Margaret Wang, *Mrs. Wishy-Washy* by Joy Cowley, and *We're Going on a Lion Hunt* by David Axtell, to reinforce early phonics and phonemic awareness skills at this phase of children's literacy learning.

Phonics (Phonological Awareness, Phonemic Awareness, and Phonics)

What we often refer to as phonics instruction can more accurately be described as phonological awareness, phonemic awareness, and phonics, including understanding the graphophonetic representation of letters. Each is integral to developing a reading process. See Scarborough's Reading Rope discussed earlier in this chapter. This part of literacy, although described differently, is included in the word reading strand of the reading rope.

Teaching phonological awareness early can help eliminate reading problems children may face in later years. Phonological awareness is, simply put, the ability to recognize the spoken parts of sentences and words. You can practice with your eyes closed. Children need to hear rhyme, alliteration, syllables in a word, and onset and rime. Phonological awareness is foundational for children to develop phonemic awareness. Phonemic awareness is the capability to notice and manipulate individual phonemes or sounds in spoken words.

One of the best ways to practice identifying rhyme is by reading many rhyming poetry and books and asking students to identify the rhyming words. This sense of story and rhythm deepens the hearing of rhyme and leads to being able to read a list of words and identify which words rhyme. Books like *Frog on a Log?* by Kes Gray, *Who's Toes Are Those?* by Jabari Asim, *Ain't Gonna Paint No More* by Karen Beaumont, and *Cool Dog, School Dog* by Debra Heiligman are regulars for identifying rhyme in my classroom.

Sometimes, confusions and concerns about a student's early reading can be sorted out by observing how students perform on phonemic awareness exercises. For example, I am currently working with a student who rarely notices the second letter in blends when she reads. She reads "tip" for "trip" and "seam" for "steam." She needs more work hearing the /r/ in /tr/ and the /t/ in /st/. Using consonant blend analogy charts, segmenting the sounds in words, and applying these strategies to book reading, she can learn that skill and keep growing as a reader.

When constructivist teachers observe students struggling with early phonemic awareness development, they can address the student's ability to hear sounds in words by using pictures (children see the image of a pig and tap /p/, /i/, /g/ with their fingers) and quick activities where students segment and blend sounds in words and learn to manipulate the phonemes.

Phonics is the ability to understand how sounds function in the written word. You have to have your eyes open. Understanding that words are made up of letters and letters represent sounds. We practice daily decoding and encoding using a sequential, systematic continuum of phonics skills as our guide.

A Word about Writing and Letter Formation

When phonics instruction includes both decoding and encoding, students learn to fluidly use phonics to read, spell, and write. Remembering letter formation as a focus for teaching in the primary grades is vital. I am often asked why we don't teach handwriting anymore in schools. My answer is always that we do teach handwriting! But we call it letter formation now. And it's still an essential part of students' literacy development.

Forming the letters correctly makes writing easier for students and decreases confusion. When kindergarten teachers pay close attention to letter formation, students get a firm foundation to support their graphophonetic understanding of print.

Constructivist teachers consistently model letter formation through:

- ◆ handwritten morning messages,
- ◆ practicing the common strokes in letters using fine and gross motor activities,
- ◆ co-created anchor charts,
- ◆ predictable charts,
- ◆ interactive charts, and
- ◆ daily modeling of how writers convey their messages by making the letters correctly so that everyone can read our important message.

In other words, constructivist teachers "share the pen" with students and make writing and letter formation a disposition the students quickly and readily adopt. Knowing their teacher is a writer who pays attention to how they make the letters makes students eager to do the same thing. This is how a disposition for writing is developed.

Each student moves through the stages of writing development by sharing the pen with their teacher and writing their own words on the page daily. Students *own* the pen through daily writing in journals, writing about their reading, and writing and drawing how they figured out their math problems.

Constructivist teachers may have students write in science logs or ask students to write their plan for center time before they choose a learning center. They regularly make thank you and birthday cards for school personnel and each other. The possibilities are endless and result in early, confident writers.

Keeping Phonics Lessons Simple

There is no set "prescription" or "one-size-fits-all" approach to phonics instruction. Many would like to tell us that there is. Still, it is common sense that ongoing, informal assessment (for example, administering a spelling inventory or a phonological awareness screener) gives teachers the necessary information regarding the next steps in phonics and phonemic awareness instruction.

Some students, such as those with dyslexia, may need more time and practice with these activities, and some, such as those who have trouble remembering what they read but have excellent phonics skills, need more time and practice with reading, discussing, and writing about continuous text.

Most importantly, constructivist teachers make phonics hands-on. In my literacy lessons, children actively sort words, use Elkonin boxes (Figure 4.3), and break words into phonemes, onset-rime, and syllables. They break words into parts by physically cutting them or with magnetic letters or word tiles. They manipulate letters and sounds in words with word ladders. Every student has their own set to manipulate. This letter and word learning is then applied to reading books, poems, and other types of print. We teach for transfer.

A constructivist teacher uses real-life, meaningful strategies to teach – even with phonics. The rule of thumb for a constructivist teacher is to keep phonics lessons brief, crystal clear, and free from confusing "aids" taught to the entire class. Sometimes I call these "phonics bird walks." For example, when we teach

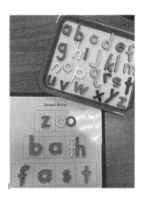

FIGURE 4.3 Tools for Phonics Instruction – Elkonin Boxes and Magnetic Letters

children that e is "bossy," it may help some students with reading CVCe words, but for others, trying to figure out whether this particular e is bossy (and how can you be silent, yet bossy?) is very confusing and makes reading harder. When my daughter learned this skill in school, I noticed she put a silent e on almost every word she wrote for a few weeks, even names, and then she figured it out.

Students have to experiment, make mistakes, sometimes overlearn concepts, and then sort them out. Teaching many arbitrary reading and writing rules, such as "bossy e" and "when two vowels go walking, the first one does the talking," can make reading confusing for some children. In my lessons, I teach students about 'silent e' and leave it at that. And I teach them that /oa/ usually says o (long o). Period. I don't expect the students to always get it right. They must experience a lot of word reading to strengthen these phonetic skills. So, I use my time to help students apply what they know about how words work, from our phonics practice to reading meaningful texts.

The Politics of Phonics Instruction
Phonics is a hot-button issue right now. Maybe it always has been. When I look at the many current phonics curricula out there – many that I have used over the years – I see a lot of consistency in each program's scope and sequence. Yet, what I see in our profession right now is widespread polarization regarding whose phonics approach is the right one. And a lot of attacking and misrepresenting others' work.

I worry that business might trump learning here. Whatever approach is beating out the others gets the profit. And unfortunately, in this case, the prize may not be our students' increased learning. It seems to be the millions of federal and state dollars that get pocketed from whatever program is currently "on top."

As constructivist teachers, we need to decide how we use these programs in our classrooms. We can't teach every student as though they have dyslexia, and we can't teach every student as though they don't have dyslexia. I've seen both approaches, and students always fall through the cracks when we are dogmatic about one view over the other.

So, let's use our common sense when it comes to phonics. Let's learn everything we can about effective phonics instruction and apply it to the instructional materials we have *and* the students we have right in front of us.

Phonics instruction is fundamental for being a reader and writer. We can approach phonics as a constructivist by knowing our children as learners, making phonics meaningful, and giving learners lots of time and practice with authentic opportunities to embed phonics in daily literacy lessons.

Example for Teaching Phonics

One of the schools where I taught employed four different phonics programs! Out of curiosity, one day, I looked at the scope and sequence of each curriculum. Nearly identical. Maybe the lessons are different, I thought. So I looked at the lessons. Two programs had daily videos to watch, and the students learned kinesthetic gestures to accompany the phonics lessons. Two of the programs had a lot of manipulatives so that the students could make words, sort words, and learn high-frequency words. The teachers had to cut out pages of words and letters for each lesson. One had a rhyme/poem to go with each letter. All had daily whole-group lessons and assessments to go along with the lessons.

After a couple of years of using all of these programs, our administration was frustrated that test scores were not significantly affected by the comprehensive approach to phonics we had employed. Students were still scoring below average on phonics and phonemic awareness on a variety of state and local assessments. "So, what's going on here?" I wondered.

I started to talk to the teachers about their phonics instruction, and the general feeling seemed to be that we had so many programs, we couldn't do them all justice. So teachers were teaching a little of this here and a little of that there – you get the idea. As I asked more questions about what the teachers felt they had time to do and what they thought they needed to leave by the wayside, I realized that they were using the more abstract aspects of the lessons, the videos, whole-group demonstrations, and independent worksheets. They were leaving out the more focused and applied aspects of the lessons, for example, using manipulatives, playing games, cooperative learning, and guided practice. The part where children experiment, practice, and self-correct was left out.

This reminds me of the Chinese proverb, "Tell me and I'll forget; show me and I may remember; involve me and I will understand!" It now made sense to me why our students weren't performing well on these assessments. We were skipping the most important parts – the shared and guided practice from Regie Routman's OLM depicted in Chapter 3. This experience illustrates the need for us to strive to make our phonics lessons as personal, concrete, and hands-on as possible.

Questions for Teaching Phonics:

- ◆ Is my phonics instruction hands-on with a lot of manipulative use or consisting more of demonstrations (including videos) and worksheets?
- ◆ Are my phonics lessons building on what students already know, or are they "one-size-fits-all"?
- ◆ Is phonics knowledge applied to reading books and writing messages?
- ◆ Do I regularly reflect on what my students know and need to know to plan my phonics whole-group, small-group, and one-on-one instruction?

REFLECTION BOX G

What questions do you have for

TEACHING PHONICS?

Vocabulary in Context (Krista)

Gone are the days of looking up vocabulary words in the dictionary (we hope). A constructivist teacher teaches vocabulary in context. The power of the read aloud includes building our language and vocabulary. In the *before* part of the read aloud, we set up the context of the book and hook our minds to what we will experience in the text. If comprehension is a concern, we set a concrete, clear purpose for reading using essential vocabulary. Write on a sentence strip or chart pad: "Read to find out…" I find using this statement before reading is astounding in its ability to help each child understand the text.

For example, "Peter sees that it's a snowy day and goes outside in the snow. We'll read to find out what happens when he comes back in from being outside in the snow." So now the students' brains are hooked. We've set them up for comprehending the text. They know the story is about Peter, who goes outside on a snowy day. And *something* happens when he comes back in from the snow. In a nonfiction book, the sentence might be, "Read to find out how camouflage can change with the environment." Now the children know their purpose for reading the text.

Students build language and vocabulary every time we read together. The cumulative effect of these conversations – every time we retell, summarize, predict, question, analyze, and notice – is a larger capacity for language and an expanded vocabulary. As a teacher, I ask, "What are you thinking now?" Or, "How did the character change?" Or, "What information is the most important under that heading?" Children are given the opportunity, time and again, to develop and increase their vocabulary, which is what increasing vocabulary requires.

Book by book, we build children's language and vocabulary. When choosing words to teach specifically, we choose critical vocabulary, those words central to understanding the text, and teach the words in-depth *after* the initial reading because the children already have the context.

For example, if I point out the vocabulary at the beginning of the story, and I'm teaching the words "picture" and "thermometer," if I introduce the words before the story is read, students may think of a picture that's on a phone or a thermometer that goes in your mouth. But in the story, the picture refers to "picture it in your mind," which means visualize. And the thermometer is the thing on the side of the house that shows how cold it is outside, not the thing I put in my mouth.

In this way, teaching vocabulary after the first reading or in subsequent readings helps children use it in context and incorporate it into their language. Here are my favorite (*after* reading) vocabulary strategies:

Critical Vocabulary Retell (Narrative/Fiction) – I learned this strategy from Pat Cunningham (2009), who has an in-depth article recalling her method called "ten vocabulary words." Jan Richardson, literacy expert, has a modified version called key vocabulary retell (2016). I love to use my version of these strategies in my classroom. In a nutshell, students use prechosen critical vocabulary cards to retell the story in sequence. In this way, each student uses a critical vocabulary word in their part of the retelling, thus incorporating the word into their language while simultaneously demonstrating comprehension of the story.

Vocabulary Boxes (Narrative/Fiction) – After reading the story, revisit key vocabulary one word at a time. Make a box on a large chart paper. Put the vocabulary word in the middle. In the upper left-hand corner, discuss and decide on a synonym that could be exchanged for that word in the story. In the upper right-hand corner, discuss and decide on an antonym for the word – the opposite of the meaning of the vocabulary. Across the bottom, write a sentence using the vocabulary word in context and draw a picture to match the sentence.

Spot the Key Words (Information/Nonfiction) – In informational nonfiction, we teach students to use a table of contents, headings, captions, text boxes, glossaries, and so on to comprehend informational text. Yet nonfiction can be chock full of new vocabulary and terminology fundamental to comprehension. Under each heading, spot one to three words essential to understanding that heading's topic. Write the words on a chart or highlight them in the text. Discuss their importance to understanding the information.

Glossary First (Information/Nonfiction) – With informational text with a glossary, read and briefly discuss the glossary first. In this activity, we are not focused on learning the words and their definitions. We are getting an introduction to what we will learn in the text. Immediately after, we have our first read of the text. On this first read, each student will flag, using colorful arrow flags, the glossary words as they come to them. Revisit each section with flagged critical vocabulary, and discuss why that word is critical to understanding the topic, making it into the all-important glossary!

Constructivist teachers build vocabulary one book, one conversation, one child, and one reading log or science log at a time. The books and dialogue in concert are the means to the end.

Example for Vocabulary in Context

I love to read aloud the accurate depiction of William from Malawi, *The Boy Who Harnessed the Wind* by William Kamkwamba (2012). Multiple reads of this text generate great rewards for the children's comprehension and knowledge of the world.

On the first two reads, learn William's contribution to Malawi and the field of science. Discuss all of the symbolism, figurative language, and short biography at the end of the book.

After the third read, introduce five vocabulary words and take turns having five children retell the story, each using the following word in their turn:

- ♦ Dreamed (William dreamed of building things.)
- ♦ Handful (William's family was starving because of the drought and only had a handful of food to eat each day.)
- ♦ Windmill (William had to drop out of school, so he checked out library books and figured out that building a windmill could produce electricity and pump water.)
- ♦ Weapon (The windmill was a weapon against drought and hunger.)
- ♦ Country (William knew that electric wind could feed his country because they could now grow food again.)

At this point, children incorporate their comprehension and key vocabulary into their own language – summarizing the text's main ideas.

Questions for Vocabulary in Context:

♦ Why is vocabulary instruction so important?
♦ When do you teach new vocabulary words? Discuss how it would change to introduce the new vocabulary words in context.
♦ What methods work for you to help children grow their vocabulary?
♦ What new methods would you like to try out in your classroom? For fiction? For nonfiction?

REFLECTION BOX H

What questions do you have for

VOCABULARY IN CONTEXT?

Reader's Theater, Book Talks, and Book Reviews (Oh, My!) (Krista)

Often, children can spend much time participating in reading instruction but only a little time actually reading. Many students need opportunities to reread texts to derive more understanding and fluency. They need more practice solving words and working out the parts of reading that are tricky for them. Reading texts more than once can be critical to constructing an effective reading process. Constructivist teachers use authentic strategies for getting students to reread familiar texts. Rather than pushing children to reread boring book passages, the following three strategies are a great place to start.

Readers' Theater

Children will reread texts over and over when they are going to perform them. I love using colorful flags to break trade books into parts. Put the book on the document presenter and go to town! Another way is to ask the students to pair up, choose a book, and break the text into parts. Now, they must read through the book to determine parts and then practice their parts. (Lots of rereading going on here!)

At first, I show students how to turn a book into a readers' theater, and we practice many times together. Then we work in pairs. Then larger groups of three or four. Sometimes, we make finger, rod, or sock puppets for the final showing. Sometimes, students bring a prop or two, such as a hat, mask, or jacket. Fridays are great for a performance day. Of course, there are many published materials with plays and readers' theater sections. It's also fun to throw those into the mix at times.

Books such as the *You Read to Me, I'll Read to You* series by Mary Ann Hoberman and Michael Emberly lend themselves to two-part readers theater. Reading the stories is a bit tricky because they rhyme, but these stories are great fun. Students can flag their parts in books with two characters as well. Books with two characters are usually easily divided into three general parts – narrator, character one, and character two. Books I love to do this with are the *Katie Woo & Pedro Mysteries* series, the *Croc and Allie* series, and the classic *Frog and Toad* and *George and Martha* series.

Book Talks

A book talk is like a book advertisement. They are fun to write and share after reading a book. Book talks are only done on books the students enjoyed, such as best friend books, independent reading books, and book series we want to share.

Here are the steps to creating a book talk:

1) Choose a GREAT book to read on your own.
2) Read the book. Then read it again, jotting down notes for your book talk.
3) Write a short description of the book, and be sure not to give away the ending – that is, unless you're in first grade or lower: little kids **can't wait** to give away the ending, and the other kids will still want to read the book!
4) Tell why you loved the book. Remember, if you didn't like the book, it's not a good candidate for a book talk.
5) Share who also might love the book.

I love asking students to script these steps and read them over a few times. This is a natural process for rereading and editing, a bonus teacher move. Students then present their book talks to the class. Video the book talks and play them wherever you can, such as parent-teacher conferences, book fairs, or in your school hallway in a prominent spot where students may often stand in line.

Before and after I read aloud to children, I often book talk a few books the students might be interested in reading on their own. Making a book sound appealing and specific to children's varied interests helps develop students into discerning readers.

Book Reviews

Older students love to give their opinions about things, right? Younger students, too, for that matter. Writing a book review differs from the old book report from my school days. It's about empowering students to give the book a personal rating or even a grade. Now, what kid wouldn't want to do that?

When we ask students to rate a book, they should justify their ratings. When students justify their ratings, they do get to share their opinions and we, as teachers, will see more of what the students comprehended from the text. When we ask children to reread a part that demonstrates their reasoning for their book ratings aloud, they are using textual evidence to back up their opinions. Younger students can share examples of characters, settings, problems, and solutions to support their opinion of a book. I have found that when I ask students to share what they think, they lean into the book a bit more.

Here is an example of reviewing books informally to engage readers. I had a reading intervention group last year of four alliterate readers. Alliterate means readers who can read, but they don't like to read. I was using a high-quality reading intervention curriculum with these students with books tailored for reading instruction and, I would say, of low to moderate interest. So, I just added a piece to each lesson where the students would "rate" the books from favorite to least favorite. Each day, we would do the phonics and syllable work, a familiar read (reread of yesterday's book), a new read, writing about reading in a reading log, and then we would rate the books and share which one we liked best and which one was the worst – and why it was the worst.

Finally, we would compare how everyone rated the books. The freedom of sharing the book ratings seemed to make the lessons more fun, and the children leaned into the lessons and grew as readers. Three of four of those readers grew out of intervention lessons midyear and were reading on grade level at the end of the year. The fourth student grew a great deal as a reader and went on to read more series and chapter books independently for the rest of the year.

After a read aloud, teachers can ask students to rate the book on a scale of 1 to 5 and explain why they gave it that rating.

1 = one of the worst books I've ever read
2 = boring, but not the worst book
3 = average book
4 = really good book
5 = one of the BEST books I've ever read

One way to complete a book review is to write a Q&A where students use class-created questions to interview each other on books they've read. Then they write up the interview as a Q&A. Many popular nonfiction books use this format, and students can learn about this literary style while publishing their book interviews into a class Q&A book.

How about rating their opinion of the author's writing style? These activities reach the highest levels of comprehension, starting with analysis or noticing aspects of the author's writing style and craft. Then moving to critique or thinking critically about the author's writing style. They can also infer the author's purpose for writing the book or analyze character changes over time or even character traits and motives. When applied to engaging books, students deepen their understanding and bring these new skills when encountering their next text.

Example for Reader's Theater, Book Talks, and Book Reviews (Oh, My!)

A challenge in today's fast-paced world of YouTube and video games is keeping students engaged in texts. I believe this has led to popular children's books having a lot less text, or word count, these days. Many excellent books are still being published, but I think they are tailored to a shorter attention span. Want to test my theory? Read the wonderful classic *The Story of Ferdinand* by Munro Leaf, or any book by Patricia Polacco, and then compare to see if you can find a current-day book with that much text and storyline.

Then again, constructivist teachers are clever and can use this to our advantage! When children do Reader's Theater, they can make stick or sock puppets and video the show with their iPads. Video your book talks and send them to parents or, even better, put them in the morning announcements. Post book reviews on a Padlet or similar app and share them with another class or school. You get the idea. Add some performance and an audience, in a social media-like manner, with a known and appropriate audience. You will see students rereading, dotting their i's and crossing their t's, and doing retakes to get it right.

Questions for Reader's Theater, Book Talks, and Book Reviews (Oh, My!):

- ◆ Why is it essential for students to reread texts?
- ◆ What texts have you reread? What was the result for you?
- ◆ What are the benefits of readers' theater, book talks, and book reviews beyond the rereading?
- ◆ How can you use a rating system to help students expand on their ideas?

REFLECTION BOX I

What questions do you have for

READER'S THEATER, BOOK TALKS, AND BOOK REVIEWS (OH, MY!)?

A Note on Teaching the Standards

While constructivist teachers help children construct their knowledge through rich classroom experiences, lessons are planned using grade-level standards as a guide. However, a constructivist teacher might not teach one standard at a time and then move on to the next. In literacy learning and literacy assessments, comprehensive reading and writing goals require students to regularly apply many standards at once.

Constructivist teachers are adept at teaching multiple standards simultaneously, meeting children where they are. For example, one child will further their understanding of the biography genre by hearing the teacher read *When Marian Sang* by Pam Munoz Ryan to a class of third graders. Another may pick up on the significance of Marian Anderson's life or the Lincoln Monument. Another child may become better at sequentially retelling a story because they remembered the critical events of this story, and so on for each student.

It is important to note all of the learning in this read-aloud example met a curricular objective or standard. Yet, instead of checking a standard off the list, the teacher opens up the conversation, knowing that they will continue to offer many opportunities to learn these concepts, regularly circling back to individual students' needs through rich, holistic learning experiences. No blanks were filled in or formulaic sentences completed. But learning happened based on what each child was ready to learn.

The Heart of Literacy in the Constructivist Classroom

Between the two of us, Dana and I have visited hundreds of classrooms over the years. Students grow exponentially in their literacy learning when they have teachers who have the instructional knowledge and skills to get to know their students' reading preferences, strengths, and needs, and then teach them where they are. We need teachers to understand how children learn to read and write; teachers who provide a myriad of literacy learning opportunities throughout each day, as discussed in this chapter; and who believe that each child can and will learn in their classroom.

5

Culturally Informed Instruction

Constructivist teachers advocate for a culturally responsive school climate. Because learning is experiential, if children are going to construct their knowledge, it starts with what the child has experienced, what they know, and who they are. Chapter 5 focuses on culturally informed instruction, nurturing authentic relationships with students, using culturally relevant resources, and reaching families with heart.

As constructivist teachers, we self-reflect on our own cultural identities to have the capacity to accept and affirm our students' identities. We understand the implicit and structural bias inherent in our society and factor social equality into our classroom curriculum and instruction. This is culturally informed teaching.

How do we ensure our teaching is culturally informed? More than checking a box each time a person of color or specific ethnicity is featured in a book or learning activity, culturally informed teaching is a belief system that permeates the school day and is included in the classroom resources, displays, book collections, units of study, guests, traditions, celebrations, and *conversations*. We embrace literature reflecting the students' "windows, mirrors, and doorways" (Bishop, 1990). As a result, children's depths of knowledge are increased by feeling seen and psychologically safe in the classroom.

DOI: 10.4324/9781032707921-6

Culturally Relevant Teaching (Krista)

I learned recently that Black History Month was originally Black History Week. It was intended to be a week to celebrate a year of learning about Black history. Since Black history was rarely included in textbooks, teachers needed to find their own materials and create a curriculum that honored the past. Eventually, Black History Week became Black History Month. Many thought this was when we taught Black history one month out of the year. We now know that, although Black History Month is a valuable celebration time, we teach Black history within a multicultural curriculum throughout the year.

BOX A   Literature Connections for the Classroom

Here are a few can't miss books for teaching Black history throughout the school year:

My Name Is York
by Elizabeth Van Steenwyk and Bill Farnsworth
York, William Clark's slave, dreams of freedom as he travels with Lewis and Clark on their 1803 Expedition.

Pies From Nowhere: How Georgia Gilmore Sustained the Montgomery Bus Boycott
by Dee Romito and Laura Freeman
The story of a hidden figure whose cooking and bravery funded a major event in the civil rights movement.

Sing a Song: How "Lift Every Voice and Sing" Inspired Generations
by Kelly Starling Lyons and Keith Mallett
This beautiful book depicts the meaning of the Black National Anthem told through personal family stories.

The Story of John Lewis
by Tonya Leslie
John Lewis's story spans the civil rights movement. Young readers will learn about the heroism of John Lewis and the major events and leaders of the civil rights movement – including a timeline and more.

The Undefeated
by Kwame Alexander and Kadir Nelson
A love poem to countless figures in Black history. Don't miss the end pages.

Teaching the traditions and celebrations of our multicultural society is important, yet more is needed. In daily lessons, we recognize our intercultural classroom, region, country, and world in inclusive examples, classroom guests, instructional materials, and literature. We do celebrate special occasions such as Black History Month, Women's History Month, Hispanic Heritage Month, and Lunar New Year; patriotic holidays such as the 4th of July, Juneteenth, Veteran's Day, Thanksgiving, MLK Jr. Day, and President's Day; holy days from our many religions; and more. Honoring these celebrations demonstrates respect for the wide diversity of our humanity.

We engage students in culturally relevant curricula to help all students understand the world we live in. In this process, students share a sense of belonging and connectedness to each other and the content we teach. Here are just a few examples of what a culturally relevant curriculum might include:

♦ We include social action in our curriculum, ensuring each student recognizes the power of their voice, and our collective voice, on issues that matter to them. Many curricular standards can be met through social action projects where students determine a situation they feel is unjust. Then they use reading, writing, math, or other content area knowledge to take action collectively, in groups, or individually.

BOX B   Literature Connections for the Classroom

Books with young people leading social action, finding their voice, and making a difference:

Change Sings: A Children's Anthem
by Amanda Gorman and Loren Long
Use music to make a change. Won't you sing along?

I Am One: A Book of Action
by Susan Verde and Peter Reynolds
One person. One small action. Each can make a difference.

Say Something!
by Peter H. Reynolds
We can all find our way to speak up because the world needs your voice.

We Are Still Here! Native American Truths Everyone Should Know
by Traci Sorell and Frane Lessac
Native American youth make presentations for Indigenous People's Day, demonstrating social action.

- ♦ In science, the videos of living scientists that lead off each science unit include a diverse collection of scientists from many fields of science. The science biographies available in our classroom offer a wide range of scientists, including hidden figures – those whose contributions to their field were not acknowledged at the time.
- ♦ School Career Day has age, gender, cultural, and racial diversity in the presenters. A wide variety of careers are represented, including family members of our students.
- ♦ Our study of the five senses includes foods, music, and artifacts from many cultural groups or regions. This helps our students know they are valued. Everyone has a place here and belongs. When learning with multicultural examples and materials, all students learn to value each other and see our similarities and differences. We are not

color blind. We see the beautiful spectrum of color, age, gender, race, region, and family structures in our world.

♦ In social studies, we encourage students to choose a historical figure to report upon and teach their contribution to society to the class. In this case, children can make the learning personal and engaging while using a variety of necessary research, organization, vocabulary, grammar, writing, and spelling skills.

♦ We hold every student to high expectations and work to differentiate our approach to learning to create a pathway to understanding for each student.

♦ When students in my classroom speak a first language different than my own, as the classroom teacher, I have an opportunity to honor that language and culture right there in my classroom. The English Learners' classroom is not the only place this happens. I can share how difficult it is to learn a language we did not grow up speaking. We can practice learning some vocabulary from another language and experience how wise we feel when we can master a few words. Imagine learning the whole language! "That is what our classmate, Emil, is learning to do. Wow." We can discuss how we can help Emil and how Emil can help us too. I can introduce and share books written in two languages.

♦ Classroom displays, bulletin boards, rituals, celebrations, and conversations are inclusive. We are communicating that the world is large with great diversity. We all belong.

BOX C   Literature Connections for the Classroom

Dual language books can bring students' home language into the classroom. Here are a few favorites:

A Is for Agbada: An African Alphabet Adventure
by Udhedhe Olakpe and Ufuoma Olakpe
Learn Nigerian vocabulary, people, places, traditions and culture through the alphabet in this celebration of Nigerian life.

Cooper's Lesson
by Sun Yung Shin and Kim Cogan
Written in Korean and English, this story explores Cooper's experience of being biracial in his family and how he learns to accept the complexities of life with the help and wisdom of an elderly store owner.

Gracias Thanks
by Pat Mora and John Parra
A Spanish-English bilingual celebration of family and all we can be thankful for.

I'll Build You a Bookcase
by Jean Coborowski Fahey and Simone Shin
Spanish-English celebration of a community that builds a variety of bookcases and shares the joy of reading every day. (Also available in Arabic-English, Mandarin-English, and Vietnamese-English.)

When We Are Kind
by Monique Gray Smith and Nicole Neidhardt
Navaho-English celebration of everyday acts of kindness.

When I travel to other countries, I have noticed that I gain experiences in two ways. I might see the new country and customs like a tourist or see the new country from the inside, more like a local. If I want to see the country like a tourist, I stay in hotels and visit restaurants that cater to Americans seeking a sense of familiarity. I pay for guided tours on buses and look out the window to see the country's dress, architecture, landmarks, and customs. If I want a local experience, I choose lodging and restaurants where the locals stay and eat. For example, if the custom is to ride a bike everywhere, I ride a bike. I experience the traditions and culture and immerse myself in everyday life. I show respect by making an effort to pronounce names, greetings, and phrases in the local language correctly.

Teaching a multicultural curriculum can feel the same way. Are we teaching the curriculum more like a tourist? Or are we immersing in the culture like a local? Constructivist teachers consider these options and work toward affirming and validating each child through understanding their culture and background.

But it's more than that. Zareta Hammond, author of *Culturally Responsive Teaching and the Brain* (2015), describes this as surface-level culture, meaning what can be seen and heard. She adds that considering our own and our students' shallow and deep culture is integral to being a culturally responsive teacher. Shallow and deep culture are the aspects of us that cannot be seen, such as our backgrounds, beliefs, worldviews, and expectations for ourselves and each other. When we examine our beliefs and biases, we can open ourselves to learning authentically, holding each of our students to high expectations for learning and ourselves to high standards for creating an environment for learning.

Classrooms become inclusive when teachers use texts and instructional practices to honor students' cultures, communities, and the world. In classroom conversations throughout the school day, a constructivist teacher welcomes and affirms the cultural diversity of the class.

Example for Culturally Relevant Teaching

One summer, when teaching a practicum for aspiring teachers, I assigned each practicum student to a kindergarten child to conduct a series of weekly interactive read alouds. The goal was for the student teachers to practice dialogic reading and then develop a unit of study around their student's interests. The university students dove into getting to know their kindergarteners and what caused that individual child to get excited about books and learning.

One day, as I observed a university student reading a range of books about trucks to her "crazy about trucks" kindergarten student, the student asked, "Do Black people drive trucks?" I think he wanted to see himself in this topic that was so exciting to him to determine if truck driving was also an option for him. The university student said, "Yes," and by the next week, she had found a range of truck books that included many gender, racial, and cultural backgrounds to share with her student.

Questions for Culturally Informed Teaching:

◆ Do I create space for sharing and learning about the culture, families, customs, and celebrations of individuals and groups in our school community?

- How does our learning environment reflect who my students are?
- How well do I know my student's cultural history and background? Do my students see their culture in our daily curriculum?
- As a culturally responsive teacher, do I ensure that every day learning and special occasions, such as Career Day, are culturally relevant?
- Do I embrace students' primary languages?
- Do I help students develop a positive racial and cultural identity?

REFLECTION BOX D

What questions do you have for

CULTURALLY INFORMED INSTRUCTION?

Windows, Mirrors, and Doorways (Krista)

Constructivist teachers embrace Rudine Sims Bishop's (1990) groundbreaking work advocating for children to be offered books that include windows, mirrors, and doorways.

Mirrors are books where I can see myself in the text and know I belong. Windows are books that show me another way of life or world I have not experienced. Doorways, sometimes called sliding glass doors, are books where I can see my path or future. Bishop advocates for multicultural and intercultural classroom literature as a means to access and equity for children. Bishop writes,

> Multicultural literature is one of the most powerful components of a multicultural curriculum, the underlying purpose of which is to help make society a more equitable one. In light of that purpose, the choice of books to be read and discussed in the nation's schools is of paramount importance.
>
> (p. 40)

As a child, I do not remember being offered books from each category, but I can look back and see that I chose texts from each category. My mirrors were books with a strong female protagonist (for their time), such as *Little Women*, *Nancy Drew*, and every Susan B. Anthony and Amelia Earhart biography I could get my hands on. My windows were books like *Charlotte's Web*, *The Lion, the Witch, and the Wardrobe*, and stories from other lands. I only read a few window books because most of the books that I had access to were written from a white-dominant cultural perspective. I read Alex Haley's epic *Roots* in ninth grade, and I believe this compelling multigenerational story greatly impacted my choice of career and region as an adult. My doorway books were all the books I read that featured strong, independent women. I wanted to be just like them when I grew up. I wanted to make my own decisions, unlike many of the women in my family whom I spent my time with as a child.

In my classroom, I have criteria I use to select books for reading instruction. I ask myself a few questions when choosing texts:

- ◆ Will this text be interesting to the students?
- ◆ Is there a representative cultural background to the students I teach?
- ◆ Is there an opportunity to learn about a wide range of cultures and communities?
- ◆ Is there an absence of stereotypes and bias?
- ◆ Have I chosen a range of genres – such as realistic fiction, fantasy, poetry, nonfiction, biography/memoir, historical fiction, mystery, action, and humor?
- ◆ Have I chosen a range of formats – such as graphic novels, odes, narrative nonfiction, chapter books, Q&A, picture books, and articles?
- ◆ For small-group reading, is the text in the student's zone of proximal development – a text where students know approximately 90%–95% of the reading skills and strategies necessary to build reading expertise and practice the 5%–10% needed to grow as a reader?

♦ For read alouds, will the text expand students' experiences, comprehension, and vocabulary?

♦ Does the book offer options I can recommend for "jumping off" into independent reading with similar books the students will enjoy?

Marion Wright Edelman, American civil and children's rights activist, said, "It's hard to be what you can't see" (2015). She was referring to the lack of representation of children of color in classroom resources and literature. Seeing ourselves represented gives us a sense of value and belonging. If children need to "see it to be it," we must provide multiple instances of culturally relevant and intercultural experiences and texts in daily instruction. For example, it is more than celebrating a popular holiday like the Day of the Dead (Dia de los Muertos); we must choose texts, including biographies, realistic fiction, historical fiction, poetry, and nonfiction, that include Hispanic people in everyday life. This honors the contribution of Hispanic people to science, industry, government, art, education, and other fields. A sense of belonging cannot be contrived. Students feel they belong when they see themselves in the classroom life and texts.

Many teachers offer these rich experiences if the classroom has Hispanic children. Now, what if my classroom has no Hispanic students? Should I leave those books out of the collection I share with children? No, I will include Hispanic cultures as a "mirror into other cultures and worlds." Honoring the cultures, languages, and customs of our regions and the world will help students to be accustomed to living in a multicultural society and not view other races, ethnicities, skin colors, and languages as "other" or as "inferior" because these different cultures are not visible in their own lives and school.

It is important to note that Mexican culture will be interesting to learn if the class includes children from many Hispanic backgrounds, such as Dominican, Honduran, Puerto Rican, and many more countries. However, each culture is unique, and it would be important to find specific Puerto Rican texts, for example, if you have students with Puerto Rican heritage.

BOX E Literature Connections for the Classroom

A few lovely books that reflect a variety of Hispanic countries and cultures:

Alma and How She Got Her Name
by Juana Martinez-Neal
Alma asks her Peruvian Daddy to tell the story of how she got her very, very long name.

Between Us and Abuela: A Family Story from the Border
by Mitali Perkins and Sara Palacios
A family travels to the U.S./Mexico border to hand gifts through the border wall to Abuela.

If Dominican Were a Color
by Sili Recio and Brianna McCarthy
A gorgeous, poetic, celebration of all of the skin tones inherent to the Dominican Republic.

Planting Stories: The Life of Librarian and Storyteller Pura Belpré
by Anika Aldamuy Denise and Paola Escobar
The story of the famous Puerto Rican librarian and storyteller who planted Spanish stories and books into New York City Libraries.

Constructivist teachers intentionally ensure that the students in their classrooms have many opportunities for windows, mirrors, and doorways in their daily learning experiences across various genres. For example, to incorporate Black culture into the classroom, teachers often read books about famous Black Americans and stories of slavery and the civil rights era. These books are essential for all students to know the reality of our American history, what has been overcome, and significant historical figures who made a difference or changed the course of history.

We also need to include books about modern Black mathematicians, architects, government leaders, poets, activists, artists, educators, and scientists. In addition, we need to share realistic fiction about contemporary Black lives, culture, opportunities, and possibilities. A variety of genres must be included, from biography, history, and historical fiction to family stories, school stories, community stories, adventure stories, fantasy, and mystery, in addition to stories with Black people from many family structures, incomes, and regions.

I am using Hispanic and Black cultures as two examples. It is essential to have representation of gender, race, age, region, economics, traditions, and family structures in our classroom experiences and literature. We also ensure the nonfiction we share includes underrepresented groups in our society.

One year, when I was a first-grade teacher, I had students from many cultural backgrounds in one class – Hispanic, Black, Hmong, white, and Native American. What a delightful year. One way that I involved all the children in learning about each other's culture was to use counting books from each heritage to learn to count in each language.

We learned to count in Spanish, Swahili, Hmong, English, and Algonquin. The children wanted to read those books over and over again. I shared a variety of multicultural literature and involved the children's families in classroom celebrations across the year. We also celebrated the unique holidays of each cultural group. I think that I was the one who learned the most during that memorable year of teaching first grade.

Every day, I observe students expressing their connection to the texts we read. Comments such as, "I live on a farm/in an apartment/with my grandparent too"; "I am Nicaraguan/Mexican/South African just like in the story"; "I play soccer/baseball/hopscotch"; "I moved to a new city/school/house too." Together, we can have rich conversations about the texts, characters, settings, and plots through questioning, analyzing characters, and critiquing shared texts' themes and content. We are not passersby; we are involved. We connect this learning to our own experience.

Remember the importance of using intercultural texts. Intercultural texts include characters from many cultures and backgrounds interacting with each other in everyday settings. These are not ambiguous characters. Their cultural backgrounds add meaning and context to the story. The range and number of published intercultural texts are expanding each year.

BOX F   Literature Connections for the Classroom

Intercultural books with rich storylines for the classroom:

I'm New Here
by Anne Sibley O'Brien
Learn how it feels to be a new student who doesn't speak English. Maria, Jin, and Fatima are all students making a new beginning in America.

The Day You Begin
by Jacqueline Woodson
There are a lot of ways we can feel different or out of place, but when you take some steps toward sharing your own story, you might meet others who want to share their story too.

The Sandwich Swap
by Kelly DiPucchio and Rania al-Abdullah
Lily and Salma, best friends, bring their lunch every day. Salma brings a hummus sandwich, and Lily brings a peanut butter sandwich. One day, they try each other's sandwiches, and a food fight erupts.

Thank You, Omu
by Oge Mora
Omu cooks a large pot of Nigerian stew. The delicious scent wafts out the window and into the neighborhood, enticing the neighbors to ask for some until it's all gone before Omu gets to have any.

Constructivist teachers use multicultural children's literature in their classrooms to help students connect with authentic characters, content, and situations rather than view people from other cultures as exotic or foreign or, worse, "other" (meaning not like me or us, not relevant). Engaging children with thoughtfully selected multicultural literature helps us all understand that we have a cultural background and story to tell, and this story is valued in our classrooms.

Example for Windows, Mirrors, and Doorways (Krista)

When my daughter was in third grade, I read her the E. B. White trio of books. We started with *Stuart Little*, a fantasy story about a mouse and his "human" adventures.

Then we read the *Trumpet of the Swan*, another fantasy story about a swan and his "human" adventures. She loved both books wholeheartedly and could not wait to read *Charlotte's Web* – another fantasy story about farm animals, especially a pig and spider, who have "human" experiences.

As we got into the first chapter or two of *Charlotte's Web*, my daughter kept stopping my reading. She was horrified to find out that Fern's father was going to kill the runt of the litter of pigs with an ax! She did not understand. In addition, early in the book, Fern's brother runs around with an air gun and hops on the school bus with it. She really did not understand that the boy had a gun and was going to take it on a school bus. Moreover, she seemed concerned that I was okay with it and still reading the book to her.

Most of us know that *Charlotte's Web* is set in the 1940s and takes place on a farm, but my daughter had difficulty comprehending this story. She is a city kid in the 21st century. She has always lived in a city and had little context in her background for that setting or time and place in rural America. Apparently, she could imagine a tiny mouse that drives a car and a swan who plays the trumpet, but *Charlotte's Web* was too much.

I offered a great deal of background knowledge, and we eventually settled into the book, enjoying the classic children's novel. Yet I wondered, if I were her teacher and read *Charlotte's Web* to my daughter, would her reaction to the text make me think she was a child without background knowledge – a child whose lack of life experience and vocabulary impaired her ability to be a strong reader in third grade? Or would I have realized that, as a city kid, my daughter does not have the context or background knowledge for this text, so I would need to build that for her and possibly many of the students? What would I have done? And how often does this happen in our classrooms?

Interestingly, the Newberry-winning *Last Stop on Market Street* was published around the same time we read *Charlotte's Web*. *Last Stop on Market Street*, written by Matt de la Peña and illustrated by Christian Robinson, is about a boy and his grandmother who take the city bus full of interesting people to serve at a soup kitchen. The figurative writing is complex and beautiful, but my daughter had no problem understanding the context of taking a city bus and going to help at a soup kitchen. She has had both of those experiences many times.

Constructivist teachers recognize that our students' life experiences may be different yet equally relevant to learning. We all need to build background knowledge in some areas of our learning, and teachers can plan instruction with that in mind.

Questions for Windows, Mirrors, and Doorways:

◆ What are your windows, mirrors, and doorways?
◆ Does every child in my classroom see themselves and each other in our classroom literature?
◆ Do I teach with a range of multicultural children's books that can be windows, mirrors, and doorways for my students?
◆ Have I included intercultural texts in my classroom literature? What can I do to add more?

REFLECTION BOX G

What questions do you have for

WINDOWS, MIRRORS, and DOORWAYS?

Reaching Families with Heart (Krista)

Constructivist teachers do not need to be experts in world cultures or history. We need to be adept at honoring and accepting each child and ensuring they can see themselves in the classroom, the literature, and the curriculum. We approach this with a spirit of curiosity as we learn about the families of the children we teach, sometimes having lifestyles and cultures that may be very different from our own. Our children must know that we value their cultures, ideas, and families. I think children easily pick up on whether the school or their teacher feels respect for their family.

As constructivists, we know our environment growing up led to our culture and beliefs as adults. We understand all people have biases due to their environments and what is known and unknown. We investigate our own biases and work through them. For example, being raised in small, homogenous, midwestern towns, my family and friend groups had been mostly people who looked like me, spoke like me, and had the same small-town traditions. When I moved to a large urban area for a teaching job after graduating from college, I had many learned stereotypes to work through about city life and the many different groups and cultures I newly encountered. These had become a part of my unconscious beliefs or biases. I wanted to feel a sense of belonging and connectedness in my new, diverse setting. I had to open my mind, read, discuss with critical friends, and understand the broader spectrum of people and lifestyles. As constructivists, we can be curious about and challenge our own beliefs while we honor each child where they are and who they are.

We expect our students to respect and embrace who we are, so of course, we respect who they are. A first step in showing this respect is by learning to say each of our students' names correctly, even when we haven't heard that name before or find it hard to pronounce. When children feel seen, they feel safe and can open their minds to learning. I am still checking my assumptions and beliefs regularly. It is part of being an open-minded teacher who embraces a culturally responsive curriculum.

One year, I had a third-grade student who honored Ramadan. Ramadan is a Muslim holy month where many Muslims fast from sunup to sundown. At the time, I did not know much about this tradition. My student, Isa, was worried about sitting in the lunchroom and not eating. I asked him if he wanted to come to the classroom for lunch. He eagerly accepted my invitation, and Isa started missing lunch the next day. Many classmates were curious, and some teased Isa that he "couldn't eat." We tried to explain, which helped some, but the children really understood once the books about Ramadan I had ordered were delivered. We were studying maps then, so I incorporated this mini-study of Ramadan into our social studies unit. Each day for a week, I read aloud a book about Ramadan, connecting it to the world map and where people who observe Ramadan live (everywhere!). We had rich discussions, and Isa felt more comfortable talking about his family's customs. Now we understood why Isa did not eat when the sun was up that month. It became just another example of how people live.

Our children all have families of origin and family stories as we do. They have ancestors, tragedies, successes, trials, and celebrations. Recently, the father of two children I teach in reading intervention died suddenly in an accident. This has affected my teaching with these two children because I am aware that they are still grieving. Sometimes I need to adjust our lessons to help them connect to their learning on particularly difficult days.

Our children love their families and traditions, which is what they know. To reach all children, we can respect their backgrounds and be willing to check ourselves for bias or lack of awareness, learn from it, and work for equity for each child.

Example for Reaching Families with Heart

Families contribute to their children's education in various ways. Almost every person in America has their own definition of what school is to them, and this can be handed down to the next generation. I think that many parents participate with schools in direct proportion to how welcomed they feel either at their children's school or how included they felt during their own school experience. We must also reach families where they are and who they are, just like the children.

Over the years, I have been one of the teachers who would complain that "the parents only come if the kids are involved in a school performance." Now, I find myself being one of those parents! I cannot be at the school volunteering in classrooms most of the time since I must be at my job. I do volunteer work and help now and then as my schedule allows, but, alas, it is usually for those things that directly involve my children.

Like me, most parents cannot be at school on a consistent basis, but I have learned that the most powerful parent involvement is to check on their children's homework, reach out to the teacher to learn about their child's progress, and consistently ask their children about what they are learning at school. It is also helpful for parents to ensure their children have access to reading and books.

Questions for Reaching Families with Heart:

♦ Do I reach out to connect with all the families of my students?
♦ Do children in my classroom feel comfortable being themselves?
♦ Do I meet families where they are (just like with students)?
♦ Do I encourage children to write about and make connections to their own lives in my instruction?

REFLECTION BOX H

What questions do you have for

REACHING FAMILIES WITH HEART?

Culturally Informed Instruction with Heart

When I was a child, I only had a handful of books at home, but I was a library kid. My family moved a lot, and the first thing

I did in each new town was find the local library. When I got old enough, I walked or biked there by myself. A single parent raised me, and I did not have many books. (I can remember three, to be exact.) But I had the library, bookmobile, and school library. Even though I did not have the traditional family structure or an involved parent at school, my family loved me. This makes me aware of how children today can be stigmatized by presuppositions about children raised by a single parent without many books in the home. I understand those children because I had a similar experience. I know that not everyone understands. This causes me to take a second look when there are things about children at school that I question or do not understand. I can check my bias, open my mind, and lean in to learn about those children.

Connecting new learning and our students' lives, experiences, and interests is a cornerstone of constructivist teaching. We work to expand our children's understanding of new ideas, the world, and its people. More than holidays, celebrations, and offering materials with diverse representation, we connect to student's daily lived experiences. We hold high expectations with support to ensure they succeed. We help students understand their world through inquiry and analysis of social issues throughout the curriculum. We make being culturally informed a priority.

6

Reconsidering Common Practices through a Constructivist Lens

Sometimes, I (Krista) wonder if every profession has as many rituals, traditions, and time-worn practices as education. We sometimes hold on to how we have always done something, even when data negates its effectiveness. A large-scale example would be our typical school year calendar. We shut down our schools in May/June and open them up again in August/September, even though it has been established that the months off in the summer lead to learning loss and food insecurity for many children.

Interestingly, one of the schools where I taught was a year-round experimental school. We were the only school in a large school district that had school year-round, ten weeks on, then one week for professional learning and a one-week break. We still had winter vacation and spring break. Families had to opt into the schedule because it was a change from tradition. This initiative showed positive student and teacher outcomes but never caught on or replicated. That is where I met Dana McMillan. She was one of our consultants in those valuable weeks of professional learning.

What about recess or homework? Both issues have received much attention in recent years. Recess had been fading from school schedules in favor of more instructional time. In light of a new understanding of how valuable recess is to students'

DOI: 10.4324/9781032707921-7

well-being and learning, the tide appears to be moving in favor of *all* students getting time to play outside.

Assigning homework is also becoming a less popular practice. Teachers were using valuable instructional minutes and hours to manage homework expectations. Without homework to manage, we can use more time for instruction and working with students at school. Parents and children can get their evenings back. All I can remember about my son's fourth-grade year is a staggering amount of homework. Two years later, when my daughter was in fourth grade, their school had examined and reconsidered the issue of homework, and my daughter had almost no homework with the exact same teachers. Although her brother was furious, the difference didn't appear to affect my daughter's learning, and the school continued to excel.

Another example is what Dana calls the hardest issue of them all: Retention. She is asked about this issue regularly and can be met with resistance to her constructivist response. Yet, the research is clear. More people of color, boys, children with learning disabilities, and children from economically disadvantaged neighborhoods are retained. In light of these inequities and often devastating results of retention policies, we hope this issue can be set aside by moving to more productive ways to recover school credits.

In this chapter, we will use a constructivist lens to explore similar issues such as rewards, grade-level teams, screen time, curriculum, and motivation. Let's see if these are areas you or your school might want to revisit.

Grade-Level Teams (Krista)

Collaborative grade-level teams can be essential to thriving as a constructivist teacher.

Consider a situation where grade-level teams structure their collaborative planning time to strengthen their teaching practices and share instructional dilemmas. This grade-level team environment has the primary purpose of supporting student growth and development.

A weekly grade-level planning time is widely utilized in schools with varying levels of success. Sometimes, these meetings are heavily facilitated by instructional coaches or school administrators. Sometimes, these meetings are ways for schools to communicate policy and expectations. Other times, teachers are free to schedule the time as needed. These meetings can become venting or sharing-the-workload sessions where teachers departmentalize the planning and preparation. For example, "I will plan the math instruction for the week, and you can plan science." In this case, little collaboration is taking place.

Here is a starter list of what we believe productive grade-level teams do:

♦ Troubleshoot lessons, units of study, and individual student progress
♦ Use student work to make informed decisions for planning future lessons
♦ Create a community of colleagues who support and care about each other
♦ Discuss observations of student progress and construct learning experiences based on these observations
♦ Adapt learning units and lessons based on student needs, interest, and inquiry
♦ Discuss data, current research, and professional articles in our field

Here is a brief list of what we believe can be unproductive for grade-level teams and children:

♦ Departmentalization, which limits ownership in our lessons
♦ Time focused on school-wide issues and communications rather than grade level and students
♦ Focused conversation on perceived student and family deficits without an action plan
♦ Focus on preparing children for the next grade rather than focusing on what they can learn now – in other words,

if we spend all year getting students ready for what second graders need to know in third grade, what happens to the year of second-grade learning?

We feel grade-level teams are essential to overall school performance, classroom learning, joy, and climate. Effective school administrators and coaches use the following practices to shape and support grade-level teams.

- ◆ Give teams a chance to move through psychologist Bruce Tuckman's stages of team development – form, storm, norm, and perform – the predictable phases each professional team moves through if they are to become high-functioning (Bonebright, 2010)
- ◆ Encourage the team to share the air in collaborative conversations and help them see the positive outcomes of their efforts
- ◆ Let the team form over time, possibly taking more than one school year to become highly productive
- ◆ Notice, document, and celebrate team accomplishments
- ◆ Let each team member determine the strengths and needs they individually bring to the group
- ◆ Listen to the team's needs and questions and then work from there using dilemmas from their daily instruction as the team's work, enabling teachers to experience time spent with their grade-level team as authentic and productive

Productive grade-level teams who reach Tuckman's level of "performing" greatly influence student achievement, school culture, and teacher longevity rates. Nurturing the grade-level team's meaningful contribution is worth the effort and attention required.

Example for Grade-Level Teams

Each grade-level team had a distinctive personality, particularly at one school where I was a teacher. I noticed that one grade-level team would regularly stand in the hallway outside their classroom doors after school, talking about their day and the students. It sounded like a venting session to me that could become very negative, and I tried to steer clear of those conversations.

Another team right down the hallway also met in the hallway after school, and their conversation topics could be similar. Still, their tone was positive, and they were careful to talk about the children in ways that led to problem-solving and appreciating different students' individuality. In this case, I often stopped to join the conversation, especially when I heard one of my reading intervention student's names brought up. I knew it would be a comfortable conversation and could help me understand that student, or even better, we would collaborate on a plan. At the time, a troubled student was coming to help me each morning if he had a good day the day before. He chose this consequence when he met with the teacher about his disruptive behavior. This collaboration came out of these after-school chats.

Students and teachers thrive and grow when grade-level teams share this constructivist approach, lifting the climate of the entire school.

Questions for Grade-Level Teams:

♦ How are teacher teams configured at your school?
♦ Have you been on an effective grade-level team? What made it effective?
♦ What can administrators do to support your teaching team?
♦ Do the grade-level teams in your school make the school better?
♦ Are there beliefs and practices regarding grade-level teams that need to be revisited?

REFLECTION BOX A

What questions do you have for

GRADE-LEVEL TEAMS?

Screen Time (Krista)

In today's classrooms, there are a lot of screens and a lot of screen time. A constructivist teacher makes many decisions about when screen time is appropriate and when it is unnecessary. We considered teaching vs. assigning in Chapter 3, which may be a good way to look at screen time. I wonder, are we teaching with screens or assigning with screens? Put another way, do we use the OLM when asking students to learn on electronic devices? If we were using the OLM, we would be demonstrating and then working collaboratively in shared and guided practice with our devices. If not, we are moving straight to independent practice by assigning.

I recently informally surveyed a group of educator friends in various school districts about their district curricular requirements for using packaged curriculum software in the classrooms. These online instructional programs are often for test prep or extra practice for math and reading. The result was so interesting. The average was about 20 minutes for a required math app and 20 minutes for a reading app. The districts offered additional materials for online learning, but these were not required daily. These were intended to enhance the curriculum when and if needed.

I had a follow-up question. I asked if they see this happening in the classrooms – approximately 40 minutes of screen time per instructional day. The overall response was that students spent much more time than that on screens each day and that this was concerning because the screen time often seemed arbitrary, as if it were a break or filler, something to do. So, how much screen time is too much?

We can go to the American Academy of Pediatrics (AAP) for some guidance. The AAP (2021) states that some types of screen time are better than others. The general rule is to look at how it engages the child. For example, there's a vast difference between 30 minutes of a child playing an online game with little educational value in an app versus 30 minutes spent creating a model for a rainforest unit of study.

According to the AAP, if a child is engaged or connected when using technology, that's better. For example, when children sing along to short educational videos, they are more actively engaged; when they are watching passively, not as much. If children are required to use critical thinking skills, such as working through dilemmas or developing a presentation, that's even better. And the best use of technology is when children are being creative by developing something new that wasn't here before.

As constructivist teachers, we pay attention to how much time children spend on screens and monitor the quality of the programs children are using. When using screens, apps, and curricular online programs with children, we ensure the learning goal is clear. When using technology, the teacher still works with the children to measure understanding, help with confusion, and discuss their learning. We might pair students while working on screens so they can talk about what they're doing and learning. We might use programs where the teacher can actively interact with the students while working in the app. We can do projects using technology and debrief the process after students' screen time learning. We let go of screen time activities that have little educational value and take up too many of our precious learning minutes each day.

Example for Screen Time

I have gone back and forth about reading and writing on classroom screens. Should we? Shouldn't we? The answer is a resounding YES. Of course, we can read books and write authentically on screens. I am doing that right now with many helpful resources at my fingertips – a thesaurus, formatting help, and *Goodreads*, among many websites I count on.

In most American schools now, every classroom includes a large screen. We need to consider this type of screen time in addition to the students' time on individual devices. When we're not aware, this amount of screen time can add up to significant minutes of mostly passive learning. I've noticed when children sit a lot during the classroom day, we often use the screen as a "brain break." And when they come in from outside recess, we might show a video to "cool down." What if we rethought this structure and didn't have children sitting so often? What if they moved around the room to various activities throughout the day? Would they still need the "downtime" of a video or the "uptime" of a brain break? It's essential to look closely at how we use our screens academically with students.

Questions for Screen Time:

◆ How do I monitor and participate in individual screen time with students?
◆ How do I use the large screen in my classroom?
◆ How much total time are students on screens each day?
◆ Where do I use screen time effectively in my classroom?
◆ Are there times when I could substitute screen time with a more interactive and engaging activity?

REFLECTION BOX B

What questions do you have for

SCREEN TIME?

Rewards (Dana)

In a constructivist classroom, students take an active role in their learning. There is an intrinsic motivation to figure something out, put effort into a project, or create something new. When rewards, often seen as a type of payment, are offered in advance, the task becomes more about extrinsic motivation. If the child does what the teacher asks, they get a reward. This may work with low-engagement tasks for a while. *However, does the promise of receiving a reward for accomplishing something meaningful make **learning** less rewarding for children?* Yes.

For any discussion on rewards, I always turn to Alfie Kohn, who writes and speaks widely on human behavior, education, and parenting. Alfie Kohn suggests our nation is fixated on rewards, contests, winners, and losers, and our schools are no exception. Reading his book, *Punished by Rewards*, revolutionized my thinking. Before that, I had always assumed that rewards were motivational. I had taken for granted that rewards were a necessary part of the school experience. It was an eye-opener, and once I began to look for the real issues with rewards, I saw exactly what he was saying.

Kohn (2018) explained,

> *Carrots, like sticks, are not merely ineffective over the long haul but often actively counterproductive – at work, at school, and at home – and these negative effects are found across ages, genders, and cultural settings. As a rule, the more you reward people for doing something, the more they tend to lose interest in whatever they had to do to get the reward. And they often end up being less successful at a task they're completing than are people who weren't offered any reward for doing it.*

(p. 278)

Rewards may take away the intrinsic motivation to do something because it is interesting, fun, or worth doing. They can take away intrinsic motivation altogether. We want to help children use their internal locus of control, not depend on getting something every time a job is done well.

Yet, praise can be different. We should praise students for their effort and a job well done. When we give students specific comments highlighting their efforts, this encourages self-assessment and builds intrinsic motivation. We can be thoughtful about how we offer praise and encouragement while we move away from rewards as a motivational tool. Here are some guidelines for praising students:

◆ Be specific about what you observe
◆ Praise what is in the child's control
◆ Give praise by asking the child how they feel about their work
◆ Acknowledge effort
◆ Make your emphasis on learning – something the child can do today that they couldn't do before

Let's keep our eyes open for how often we reward students and consider whether we can reduce some of these practices and increase opportunities for intrinsic motivation that gives the child control over their accomplishments.

Example for Rewards

One day, I arrived early for a professional development session at an elementary school to find the school administrators, teachers, and students gathered in the gymnasium. The principal was conducting a meeting with the students who would soon begin taking the required state test. He announced with great fanfare that the school board had approved, just like last year, that all students who scored proficient or above would receive $40 for each test section.

Shortly after his announcement, one boy raised his hand and was called on by the principal. His question was, shouldn't they get more this year if they received $40 last year? The boy suggested $50 with great enthusiasm from the other students. This is one of the problems with rewards. We will always want more, and we create a situation where students often do the minimum required to receive the reward rather than doing their best.

Here are a few more examples of practices focused on extrinsic motivation we might reconsider:

◆ Offering prizes and rewards for test scores
◆ Offering rewards for doing daily schoolwork
◆ Rewarding students for attendance when parents most often control young children's attendance. Other examples reliant on parents include rewarding children for being on time, paying for field trips, and completing home reading logs, all areas where the child may not have much control
◆ Rewarding when children do the minimum to reach their reading and math learning goals rather than use their regular motivation to learn and grow
◆ Taking away recess from the children who find it hard to stay in their seats or focus – the children who may need it the most

- Offering rewards for reading a preset number of pages or books or completing a set number of challenging math problems
- Showcasing students' names who have achieved a set benchmark for accomplishment on a state or local standardized test

What about celebrating learning or successes? A celebration can feel different because there wasn't a predetermined offer. It is a post-activity event that wasn't tied to a reward. The same reward, given as a celebration and not used as an incentive or contingent on complying with a request, is seen differently by the child. Rewards change the locus of control, taking the power from the student and placing it in the hands of the one who rewards. Appreciation, on the other hand, is not seen as a reward. It is more likely to be seen as a personal acknowledgment of the effort given.

Students are motivated when given the agency to make learning and personal achievement the most important thing. I believe in helping children do the right thing because it is the right thing to do. Rewards rob them of this mindset. It can send an unintended message to students and parents about the values of our school.

Questions for Rewards:

- What do you think about using praise and reward systems?
- How can we praise children for their efforts and accomplishments in a way that supports their intrinsic motivation?
- When did you use a reward system that did not work? Why did it not work?
- What has happened when you have tried out a reward system?

REFLECTION BOX C

What questions do you have for

REWARDS?

Curriculum (Dana)

We all have grade-level curricula to follow in our state and school districts. Just the word "curriculum" can have different meanings for different educators. Do we mean the standards, the adopted resources and materials, a pacing guide, or general developmental guidelines for learning? Whatever our understanding, curricula are written with the intention of meeting the needs of all learners. As constructivists, we want to add that these needs don't have to be met on the same day and in the same way.

Sometimes, with our intent of following the curriculum and ensuring children receive the same instruction, teachers are expected to be on the same lessons at the same time. With this method, teachers simply follow the lessons and teach the skills to the whole group. This common practice attempts to teach to the center, ensuring every child has access to the entire curriculum. We understand that. However, we worry that if the written curriculum dictates daily teaching and learning, many children will not get the instruction they need when they need it.

When discussing how to meet children where they are, the question of whether constructivist teachers have high expectations for learning always emerges. Yes, we do have high expectations for all children. In fact, we believe balancing the curriculum with the individual student is the only way for students to meet high expectations for learning.

The learning theory presented by Lev Vygotsky, a Russian psychologist and prominent education researcher, is the basis for our work. Vygotsky's research demonstrated that students have learning zones – including what can't be done right now, what can be done independently, and what can be learned right now with scaffolding and support. Vygotsky (1978) defined these stages as the zone of achieved development and the zone of proximal development. He defined the zone of proximal development as "the distance between the actual developmental level as determined by independent problem solving and the level of potential development as determined through problem solving under adult guidance or in collaboration with more capable peers" (p. 33).

In other words, teaching in the zone of proximal development means teaching to the highest level the student can meet with support right now. We scaffold student learning from the zone of proximal development to the zone of achieved development, or what the student can do independently. Then we move to the next advanced step, which has become the new zone of proximal development. From here, we continue the cycle of scaffolded teaching, moving to the next challenge guided by the child's learning. This is how we have high expectations for each student's individual growth. We know the student as a learner, monitor their progress, and adjust our teaching as necessary. In essence, we make sure all children get the instruction they need so they can incrementally learn and grow to meet our *high expectations*. See Figure 6.1.

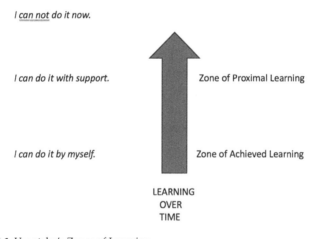

FIGURE 6.1 Vygotsky's Zones of Learning

Let's look at the role of the curriculum from a constructivist perspective. Having every student working on the same lessons does not make as much sense when considering each child's development. Therefore, constructivist teachers can make a shift and use the curriculum as a *guide*. We pull the broader idea out of the curriculum and differentiate within those concepts, meeting the more specific needs of each learner. When we do this, we are less likely to teach over the students' heads, causing frustration, or teach content students already know, causing boredom.

Here is an example of what can happen when only the curriculum directs the lesson planning. One day, I visited a school to observe and support the teachers in their math instruction. On the day of my visit, the math curriculum called for an introduction to division. The teacher placed the students into three small groups. She called the first group to her teaching table. She briefly introduced the idea of division and showed the group a chart with the sequence of steps for solving a division problem. (This is not how a constructivist would start a unit on division.)

The first group appeared to be challenged by this new process of dividing. They followed the steps on the first problem presented and, with some coaching, arrived at the answer. They worked through a couple more problems together and were then returned to their desks with a worksheet of more long division problems to do alone. Again, this is not a constructivist approach.

The second group arrived at the teaching table, and the teacher followed the same procedure but without the same results. This group appeared confused by what they were to do and why they were doing it. They became lost in the steps, and in the end, they were frustrated. It was clear that many of the students in this group needed more fluency in their multiplication tables; thus, in the division problem, these errors made the final result incorrect. The teacher gave the students the same worksheet at the end of the lesson. I wasn't sure how they would manage the worksheet.

Finally, the teacher called the third group to the table. The lesson was similar to the second group; only this group of students could not subtract or multiply. Some students ended up in tears, and when the students were out of the room, the teacher ended up in tears too. I didn't blame her. You cannot do long division when you need to learn to multiply or subtract.

The curriculum may have called for this lesson, but it was only a fit for some of these 9-year-olds. Curriculum designers will tell us that math will spiral through the concepts, and the students who did not understand it the first time will have other opportunities. My concern is that when students have another opportunity to learn division, they will build their learning on the confusions they experienced during this first go around. And the students may feel like they can't do math, which is a problem much harder to correct.

By putting the child first, we put our effort into planning the next steps that make sense to the child. We use the curriculum to plan lessons that are in the student's zone of proximal development. With the overarching goal of dividing, we can go back to work on the part necessary to get there in small groups. In math, students typically develop number sense before addition, addition before subtraction, and subtraction before multiplication. Then, they will be ready to tackle division.

Constructivists teach number sense if the child needs number sense before being ready to do addition. They use manipulatives and math games requiring number sense. They help students make drawings of their mathematical thinking and read books about numbers. They do not stop until the child has developed number sense and is ready to do addition, confident in their abilities, and excited to move on to a new math concept.

When teaching broader ideas, we can attend to students' next steps in our lessons without teaching everyone the same lesson every day, whether they need it or not. Flexible groups, projects, individual coaching, and learning stations are so important in this type of teaching. The teacher becomes a facilitator of students getting the instruction that will propel them forward.

Example for Curriculum

How would a constructivist teach division? Constructivists teach a new math concept by allowing students to explore the purpose: Why do we need this skill? They do not begin with the traditional steps, as the teacher in my example did. They begin by considering the purpose of division. You might ask the students what they would do if they had a whole bunch of items and needed to distribute them equally.

Here is one way you could introduce division. Begin this lesson with a bag of goldfish crackers. Tell the students that you will distribute the crackers equally to each of them, but you need help figuring out how many each will receive. Count the crackers first and print the number on a whiteboard or chart paper. Remind the students that this is the total number of crackers that will be divided between them. Write down the number of students in the group to the left of the total number. Then, ask, "How many crackers will each of you receive?"

Get a very calm look on your face, take a few deep breaths, and allow them to work out how they would do it. When you embrace this step, you will find it very interesting to see how each student approaches this problem, and they have a vested interest in finding the solution – an equal number of crackers!

Some students will make drawings; some may use manipulatives to create the problem. Any way they approach the problem is fine. They are working out a multitude of concepts. Let them work through the process. When everyone has arrived at an answer, the next level of learning begins when we compare the answers. Avoid correcting or judging the answers and allow students to discuss their various answers and how they arrived at them. Encourage debate, a wonderful constructivist tool for helping students consider their thinking and adjust their ideas. When students explain how they arrived at their answers, they sometimes correct their own mistakes in the process.

Once the class arrives at a conclusion everyone agrees on, test their theory by distributing the crackers. This process will take time, and depending on their skill level, you may need to repeat it for several days with a new and practical problem for them to solve. Each of them must be secure in their understanding of the concept.

When students are taught the steps to a process without a conceptual understanding, they are lost if they get confused or forget their one strategy. With a clear concept about what they are doing, children have multiple ways they can always depend on to approach the problem.

Teaching students before they're ready is like building a house with no foundation. Those foundational skills support the new learning, and the curriculum can guide this process, but it takes a knowledgeable teacher to know what students need next. The decisions we make every day for those 180 or so days of school make the difference for children.

Questions for Curriculum:

- ♦ How do you define curriculum?
- ♦ Do you have students who need help with a current math concept? Consider when and how they became lost and what foundational skills they may need.
- ♦ How do you introduce a new math concept? Subtraction? Double-digit subtraction? Fractions?
- ♦ What can you do to make the new concepts real for students?

REFLECTION BOX D

What questions do you have for

CURRICULUM?

Motivation (Krista)

What if we helped children feel invited to learn rather than instructed, directed, or demanded? It may sound like a discrepancy without a difference, but I think there is a significant difference. Think about a community or club you belong to, such as a biking group, a class, a team, or maybe your extended family. If your group activities were always dictated and prescribed, that would not seem very interesting or fun. Still, if your group weighs decisions about your activities together, you often have a chance for input, and you can enter the group's "work" on your terms; there is a much better chance for you to want to belong to this group.

If, on the other hand, activities are always directed and prescribed to you, you may lose interest in the group or need a large number of extrinsic rewards to keep your membership meaningful to you by doing the least amount of activity to earn the reward and then forgetting about it the minute the task is finished, and the reward is received.

Constructivists believe motivation drives learning, and the teacher's role is to tap into what children know to build on that knowledge. We often say to children, "Did you do your work?" We say it in good faith, understanding that we are asking if the child did their learning task. Nevertheless, when anything feels like work, it is less fun, less likely we will enjoy the work, and we will be less likely to want to do it again. In this way, school can feel like drudgery – a place without agency or fun.

However, what if children felt the work was fun? Moreover, what if they had some choice for what the work would entail or how they could go about it? When children feel invited to the learning rather than directed, we honor their role and help them see learning as an opportunity.

We can invite children to sit on the carpet and share a story. We can invite children to share their thoughts about the learning activity. We can invite children to "rate" the book we have read based on their favorite or least favorite. We can invite children to choose where they work, such as on the floor, at the table, or at their own desk or workspace. By honoring the child's own inclinations for how they like to learn, we show them how we value their ideas. We honor that this is their classroom and their learning journey.

Example for Motivation

When I taught third grade, I noticed that many teachers used a process of memorizing multiplication facts and then gave a cut-out of a scoop of ice cream when each multiple was mastered. Teachers would assess students' aptitude for each multiple by having students write out their multiplication facts in one minute or less, usually starting with the 2s and working up through the 12s.

This process concerned me because I wasn't sure if children understood that 4 x 6 meant four groups of six items – the concept of multiplication. So, I decided to make learning multiplication facts a more developmental process. I wanted my students to spend time learning and practicing the concept before giving them a timed assessment.

I taught the students various games and manipulative activities. I had the students thinking of natural sets – such as tires in sets of four on cars and five fingers on each hand. I even read a book called *7×9 Equals Trouble* by Claudia Sims, a short chapter book perfect for helping students relieve their anxiety about multiplication facts. It is about a third grader who is more interested in social studies and science topics trying to learn multiplication facts. At the same time, his little kindergarten brother understands the concept and can rattle multiplication facts off more quickly than the main character can.

After introducing all these different ways to understand multiplication and multiplication facts, I invited the students to share which makes the most sense. I asked them to demonstrate their best way of learning multiplication facts. I found that the students always learned the facts with this approach. It has a lot to do with learning multiplication facts in many ways and then choosing what worked best for them.

Questions for Motivation:

- ♦ When have you felt invited to learn in your life or school?
- ♦ What are some ways you can invite children to learn in your classroom?
- ♦ How can your school make all teachers and students feel invited to learn?
- ♦ Are there common practices regarding motivation that need to be revisited?

REFLECTION BOX E

What questions do you have for

MOTIVATION?

The Heart of Our Beliefs

This chapter addressed a few common educational practices where our work can be reconsidered. We invite you to add some of your own topics you feel should be revisited. Teaching is a dynamic profession where research and practice are continually evolving. It truly is an art and a science. Bringing these two elements of teaching together is the hallmark of a constructivist teacher.

As we grow as teachers through experience, we continue to construct our knowledge base. We change some things we do because now that we know better, we do better. Some beliefs and practices are set down, and others are picked up and integrated into our current classroom structure. And so it goes over the long and winding road of a teaching career.

Conclusion

From Our Teachers' Hearts to Yours

We wrote this book from our hearts as constructivists who continue to learn and grow as educators every day. Our purpose was to open up the conversations we've been having over decades to include you, our readers. Talking about our important work is one of the most exciting aspects of teaching. Through our conversations, we continue to challenge our own beliefs and practices, always keeping the focus on children. We aren't trying to make each other agree – that wouldn't have kept our conversation going over the years. What has kept it going is that we are trying to get to higher ground in our beliefs together.

We each have so many beloved books and authors of our own that we've shared and discussed over the years. They ground our discussions. As colleagues and friends, we have learned that it is our conversations about teaching and learning that reassure us that our beliefs are valid and from our hearts.

Each essay, written by one of us, was one that we felt passionate about and worthy of including as a vital aspect of constructivist teaching from the heart. When the other person read and edited the essay, we discussed it in depth to be confident that it was our best. Many of the personal examples shared are ones we have used with educators in the professional development sessions we have conducted over many years.

DOI: 10.4324/9781032707921-8

It is the questions following the examples that we feel can move our discussions forward. If used in professional development sessions, the questions may help you get to the heart of your beliefs. We hope they lead to conversations between colleagues and help you create more examples to develop your beliefs. We have included our emails in the bios so you can share your questions with us.

Education is always challenging. We are constantly under stress by others who think they know better, have a better method, or a better way of conducting school – those "silver bullet" ideas that keep coming. Finding like-minded people is not easy. Having conversations around complex topics is even more challenging. But it's worth it, and this is what highly effective teachers do.

When the conversations become more difficult, we, as constructivist teachers, go to one place for guidance – the child. What is best for the children? What will make learning a joy for a child? What will touch their heart? The child is where our loyalty lies.

We want to conclude with a few lines adapted from a poem by Chilean poet Gabriela Mistral, often recited by Dr. Ernest Boyer, the late commissioner of education under the George H. W. Bush administration and then president of the Carnegie Foundation for the Advancement of Teaching. Dr. Boyer, who kept children at the center of his work, made a profound impact on each of our education journeys.

> Many things we need can wait.
> The child cannot.
> Now is the time his bones are being formed,
> her blood is being made;
> his mind is being developed.
> To her, we cannot say tomorrow,
> his name is today.

Bibliography

Afflerbach P. (2022). *Teaching readers (not reading): Moving beyond skills and strategies to reader-focused instruction*. New York: Guildford Press.

American Academy of Pediatrics, (2021, May 21). *Screen Time Guidelines*. https://www.aap.org/en/patient-care/media-and-children/center-of-excellence-on-social-media-and-youth-mental-health/social-media-and-youth-mental-health-q-and-a-portal/middle-childhood/middle-childhood-questions/screen-time-guidelines/

Aubrey K. & Riley A. (2022). *Understanding and using educational theories* (3rd ed.). Sage Publications.

Beck I. L. McKeown M. G. & Kucan L. (2013). *Bringing words to life: robust vocabulary instruction* (2nd ed.). Guilford Press.

Bishop, Rudine Sims. (1990). Mirrors, windows, and sliding glass doors. *Perspectives*, 6 ix–xi.

Blevins W. (2017). *A fresh look at phonics grades K-2: common causes of failure and 7 ingredients for success*. Corwin Literacy.

Blevins, W. (2019). Meeting the challenges of early literacy phonics instruction (Literacy leadership brief). *International Literacy Association*. Retrieved from https://www.literacyworldwide.org/statements

Bonebright D. A. (2010). 40 years of storming: a historical review of Tuckman's model of small group development. *Human Resource Development International* 111–120. https://doi.org/10.1080/13678861003589099

Boyer, E.L. (1995). *The basic school: a community for learning*. Princeton, N.J. The Carnegie Foundation for the Advancement of Teaching.

Brillante P. (2023). *Developmentally appropriate practice in early childhood programs serving children from birth through age 8*. National Association for the Education of Young Children.

Burkins J. M. & Yaris K. (2023). *Who's doing the work?: how to say less so readers can do more*. Routledge.

Burkins J. M. & Yates K. (2021). *Shifting the balance: 6 ways to bring the science of reading into the balanced literacy classroom*. Stenhouse.

Campbell S. (2021). What's happening to shared picture book reading in an era of phonics first? *Reading Teacher*, 757–767.

Cassetta G. (2013). *No more taking away recess and other problematic discipline practices*. Heinemann.

Clay, M.M. (2001). *Change over time in children's literacy development*. Portsmouth, NH: Heinemann.

Collins K. & Bempechat J. (2017). *No more mindless homework*. Heinemann.

Copple C. Bredekamp S. Koralek D. G.. & Charner K. (2013). *Developmentally appropriate practice: focus on preschoolers*. National Association for the Education of Young Children.

Copple C. Bredekamp S. Koralek D.G.. & Charner K. (2014a). *Developmentally appropriate practice: focus on kindergartners*. National Association for the Education of Young Children.

Copple C. Bredekamp S. Koralek D.G.. & Charner K. (2014b). *Developmentally appropriate practice: focus on children in first second and third grades*. National Association for the Education of Young Children.

Crothers, L. M., et al. (2010). A preliminary study of bully and victim behavior in old-for-grade students: Another potential hidden cost of grade retention or delayed school entry. *Journal of Applied School Psychology*, 26(4), 327–338.

Cunningham P. M. (2009). *What really matters in vocabulary: research-based practices across the curriculum*. Pearson.

Cunningham, P. (2005), If They Don't Read Much, How They Ever Gonna Get Good?. *The Reading Teacher*, 59: 88–90. https://doi.org/10.1598/RT.59.1.10

Davis B. M. (2012). *How to teach students who don't look like you: culturally responsive teaching strategies* (2nd ed.). Corwin Press.

Duke N. K. & Cartwright K. B. (2021). The science of reading progresses: communicating advances beyond the simple view of reading. *Reading Research Quarterly*, 25–44.

Edelman M. W. (1993). *The measure of our success: a letter to my children and yours*. Harper.

Elkind D. (1987). *Miseducation: preschoolers at risk*. Knopf: Distributed by Random House.

Elkind D. (2001). *The hurried child: growing up too fast too soon* (3rd ed.). Perseus Pub.

Ensley, A., & Rodriguez, S.C. (2019). Annotation and agency: teaching close reading in the primary grades. *The Reading Teacher*, 73(2), 223–229. https://doi.org/10.1002/trtr.1812

Fisher D. Frey N. & Hattie J. (2016). *Visible learning for literacy grades k-12: implementing the practices that work best to accelerate student learning*. Corwin.

Fisher, D., & Frey, N. (2019). Practice Makes Learning Permanent. *The Reading Teacher*, 73(3), 381–384. https://doi.org/10.1002/trtr.1857

Fountas I. C. & Pinnell G. S. (2017). *Guided reading: responsive teaching across the grades* (2nd ed.). Heinemann.

Fox M. & Horacek J. (2001). *Reading magic: how your child can learn to read before school and other read-aloud miracles*. Pan Macmillan.

Gestwicki C. (2017). *Developmentally appropriate practice: curriculum and development in early education* (6th ed.). Cengage Learning.

Graham S. & Hebert M. (2011). Writing to read: a meta-analysis of the impact of writing and writing instruction on reading. *Harvard Educational Review*, 710–744.

Hammond Z. & Jackson Y. (2015). *Culturally responsive teaching and the brain: promoting authentic engagement and rigor among culturally and linguistically diverse students*. Corwin.

Holt N. & Green S. (2010). *Bringing the high scope approach to your early years practice* (2nd ed.). Taylor & Francis.

Hudson A. K. (2016). Get them talking! using student-led book talks in the primary grades. *Reading Teacher*, 221–225.

Hughes, J. N., Kwok, O., & Im, M. H. (2013). Effect of retention in first grade on parents' educational expectations and children's academic outcomes. *American Educational Research Journal*, 50(6), 1336–1359.

Hughes, J. N., West, S. G., Kim, H., & Bauer, S. S. (2018). Effect of early grade retention on school completion: A prospective study. *Journal of Educational Psychology*, 110(7), 974–991.

Iaquinta A. (2006). Guided reading: a research-based response to the challenges of early reading instruction. *Early Childhood Education Journal*, 413–418.

Inhelder, B., & Piaget, J. (1958). *The growth of logical thinking from childhood to adolescence*. New York: Basic Books.

International Dyslexia Association. (2018). Scarborough's reading rope: A groundbreaking infographic. *The Examiner*, **7**(2). Retrieved from https://dyslexiaida.org/scarboroughs-reading-rope-a-ground breaking-infographic/

Jensen, E. (2005). *Teaching with the brain in mind* (2nd ed.) ASCD.

Katz, L. G. (1995). Dispositions in early childhood education. In L. G. Katz (Ed.), *Talks with teachers of young children. A collection.* Norwood, NJ: NAEYC.

Katz, L.G., & D. McClellan. (1997). *Fostering children's social competence: The teacher's role.* Washington, DC: NAEYC.

Katz, L.G., & J.H. Helm. (2001). *Young investigators: The project approach in early years.* New York: Teachers College Press; and Washington, DC: NAEYC.

Katz, L.G., & J. Raths. (1985). Dispositions as goals for education. *Teaching and Teacher Education, 1(4)*, 301–307.

Kelly, L. B. & Djonko-Moore, C. (2022). What does culturally informed literacy instruction look like? *Reading Teacher*, 567–574.

Kirk, E.W., & P. Clark. (2005). Beginning with names: Using children's names to facilitate early literacy learning. *Childhood Education 81*(3), 139–144.

Kohn, A. (2000). *The case against standardized testing: raising the scores ruining the schools.* Heinemann.

Kohn, A. (2018). *Punished by rewards: The trouble with gold stars, incentive plans, A's, praise, and other bribes* (25th Anniversary Edition). Houghton, Mifflin and Company.

Konrad, M.H. (2023). The love of the book: students' text selection and their motivation to read. *Read Teach.* https://doi.org/10.1002/trtr.2246

Lambert, L. (2002). *The constructivist leader* (2nd ed.). Teachers College Press; National Staff Development Council.

Laminack, L. (2016). *The ultimate read-aloud resource: making every moment intentional and instructional with best friend books.* Scholastic.

Laminack, L. N., & Stover, K. (2019). *Reading to make a difference: using literature to help students speak freely think deeply and take action.* Heinemann.

Layne, S. L. (2023). *In defense of read-aloud: sustaining best practice.* Routledge. https://doi.org/10.4324/9781032681290

Lipsey, M. W., Farran, D. C., & Durkin, K. (2018). Effects of the Tennessee prekindergarten program on children's achievement and behavior through third grade. *Early Childhood Research Quarterly*, 155–176. https://doi.org/10.1016/j.ecresq.2018.03.005

Marinak, B. A., & Gambrell, L. B. (2016). *No more reading for junk: best practices for motivating readers.* Heinemann.

McGee, L.M., and Schickedanz, J.A. (2007), Repeated interactive read-alouds in preschool and kindergarten. *The Reading Teacher*, 60: 742–751. https://doi.org/10.1598/RT.60.8.4

McNair, J. C., & Edwards, P. A. (2021). The lasting legacy of Rudine Sims Bishop: mirrors windows sliding glass doors and more. *Literacy Research: Theory Method and Practice* 202–212.

McNair, J.C. (2007). Say my name, say my name! Using children's names to enhance early literacy development. *Young Children 62*(5), 84–89.

Michaels, S., O'Connor, C., & Williams-Hall, M. C., with Resnick, L. B. (2010). *Accountable Talk sourcebook: For classroom conversation that works.* Pittsburgh, PA: Institute for Learning, University of Pittsburgh. http://ifl.pitt.edu/index.php/educator_resources/accountable_talk

Miller, D. (2013). *No more independent reading without support.* Heinemann.

Mistral, G. (1946). *Llamado por el Nino (The Call for the Child)*, Speech given to the United Nations documented by Reynaldo C. Aguirre, the Library of Congress, personal communication, 27 July 1995. * *Various translations have been made of this work. The Nobel Prize winner, Gabriela Mistral, a Chilean poet and educator, first recited this prose in a worldwide radio broadcast of the United Nations calling on people in all countries to contribute a day's salary for the benefit of children. This is believed to be the beginning of UNICEF, the United Nations International Children's Emergency Fund.*

Mistral, G. & Le Guin, U. K. (2003). *Selected poems of Gabriela Mistral.* University of New Mexico Press.

Moats, L.C., & Tolman, C. (2009). *Language essentials for teachers of reading and spelling.* Boston, MA: Sopris West Educational Services.

Moller, K. J. (2016). Creating diverse classroom literature collections using Rudine Sims Bishop's conceptual metaphors and analytical frameworks as guides. master teacher. *Journal of Children's Literature*, 64–74.

Mullick, N. (2012). Caine's Arcade [Video]. *YouTube.* https://www.youtube.com/watch?v=faIFNkdq96U

Neuman, S. B., & K. Roskos. (2005). Whatever happened to developmentally appropriate practice in early literacy? *Young Children*, 60 (4), 22–26.

Nichols, M. (2008). *Talking about text: guiding students to increase comprehension through purposeful talk*. Shell Education.

Noyes, D. (2000). *Developing the disposition to be a reader: The educator's role*. Clearinghouse on Early Education and Parenting.

Ou, S., & Reynolds, A. J. (2010). Grade retention, postsecondary education, and public aid receipt. *Educational Evaluation and Policy Analysis, 32*(1), 118–139.

Parkes, B. (2000). *Read it again!: Revisiting shared reading*. Routledge. https://doi.org/10.4324/9781032682167

Piaget, J. (1936). *Origins of intelligence in the child*. London: Routledge & Kegan Paul.

Piaget, J. (1957). *Construction of reality in the child*. London: Routledge & Kegan Paul.

Piaget, J., & Cook, M. T. (1952). *The origins of intelligence in children*. New York, NY: International University Press.

Pikulski, J.J., & Chard, D. J. (2005). Fluency: Bridge between decoding and reading comprehension. *The Reading Teacher, 58(6)*, 510–519. https://doi.org/10.1598/RT.58.6.2

Pinnell, G. S. & Fountas, I. C. (2009). *When readers struggle: teaching that works*. Heinemann.

Pion, G. M. & Lipsey, M. W. (2021). Impact of the Tennessee voluntary prekindergarten program on children's literacy language and mathematics skills: results from a regression-discontinuity design. *Aera Open*. https://doi.org/10.1177/23328584211041353

Rasinski T. V. (2012). Why reading fluency should be hot. *Reading Teacher*, 516–522.

Ravitch, Dianne, "Common care standards" dianeravitch.net Dianne Ravitch's blog, January 23, 2021.

Resnick, L. B., Asterhan, C. S. C., & Clarke, S. N. (Eds.). (2015). *Social-izing intelligence through academic talk and dialogue*. Washington, DC: American Educational Research Association.

Richardson J. (2016). *The next step forward in guided reading: an assess-decide-guide framework for supporting every reader*. Scholastic.

Richardson, J. & Dufresne Michèle. (2019). *The next step forward in word study and phonics*. Scholastic.

Robertson, D. A., & Padesky, C. J. (2020). Keeping Students Interested: Interest-Based Instruction as a Tool to Engage. *The Reading Teacher*, 73(5), 575–586. https://doi.org/10.1002/trtr.1880

Roth, K. & Dabrowski, J. (2016). *Interactive writing: a small practice with big results prek-5*. Stenhouse Publishers; International Literacy Association.

Routman, R. (1999). *Conversations: strategies for teaching, learning, and evaluating*. Portsmouth, NH: Heinemann.

Routman, R. (2003). *Reading essentials: the specifics you need to teach reading well*. Portsmouth, NH: Heinemann.

Routman, R. (2004). *Writing essentials: raising expectations and results while simplifying teaching*. Portsmouth, NH: Heinemann.

Scarborough, H. (2001) "Connecting early language and literacy to later reading (dis)abilities: Evidence, theory, and practice." In S. B. Neuman & D. K. Dickinson (eds.), *Handbook for research in early literacy*, 97–110. New York: Guilford Press.

Seidenberg, M. S., Borkenhagen, M. C., & Kearns, D. M. (2020). What's the fuss about phonics and word study? *Journal of reading recovery*, Spring, 15–26.

Siegler, R. S., DeLoache, J. S., & Eisenberg, N. (2003). *How children develop*. New York: Worth.

Sternberg, R. J. & Grigorenko, E. L. (1999). *Our labeled children: What every parent and teacher needs to know about learning disabilities*. Perseus Books.

Tingle, L. R., Schoeneberger, J., & Algozzine, B. (2012). Does grade retention make a difference? *The Clearing House, 85*(5), 179–185.

Tomlinson, C. A. (2017). *How to differentiate instruction in academically diverse classrooms* (3rd ed.). ASCD.

Trelease, J. (2013). *The read-aloud handbook* (7th ed.). Penguin Books.

Vygotsky, L. S. (1978). *Mind in society: The development of higher psychological processes*. Cambridge, MA: Harvard University Press.

Wadsworth, B. J. (2004). *Piaget's theory of cognitive and affective development: Foundations of constructivism*. New York: Longman.

Wilson, V. L., & Hughes, J. N. (2006). Retention of Hispanic & Latino students in first grade: Child, parent, teacher, school, and peer predictors. *Journal of School Psychology, 44*, 31–49.

Wood, C. (2017). *Yardsticks: Child and adolescent development ages 4–14* (4th ed.). Center for Responsive Schools.

Wright Edelman, Marian "It's hard to be what you can't see." https://www. childrensdefense.org/child-watch-columns/health/2015/its-hard-to-be-what-you-cant-see/ChildWatchColumn. Children's Defense Fund, August 21, 2015.

Wu, W., West, S. G., & Hughes, J. N. (2008). Short-term effects of grade retention on the growth rate of Woodcock-Johnson III broad math and reading scores. *Journal of School Psychology*, *46*, 85–105.

Bibliography of Children's Literature Cited

Agee, J. (2015). *It's only Stanley*. Dial Books for Young Readers is an imprint of Penguin Group.

Alexander, K., & Sweet, M. (2019). *How to read a book*. Harper an imprint of Harper Collins Publishers.

Alexander, K., & Nelson, K. (2019). *The undefeated*. Versify Houghton Mifflin Harcourt.

Anderson, D. (2018). *Croc and Ally: Friends forever*. Penguin Workshop an imprint of Penguin Random House.

Arnosky, J. (2011) *Thunderbirds: Nature's flying predators*. Union Square Kids.

Asim, J., & Pham, L. (2019). *Whose toes are those?* New York: LB Kids.

Axtell, D. (2006). *We're going on a lion hunt*. Houghton Mifflin.

Beaty, A., & Roberts, D. (2013). *Rosie revere engineer*. Abrams Books for Young Readers.

Beaumont, K., & Catrow, D. (2005). *I ain't gonna paint no more!* Houghton Mifflin Harcourt.

Bemelmans, L. (1967). *Madeline*. Viking Press.

Bingham, K. L., & Zelinsky, P. O. (2013). *Z is for moose*. Scholastic.

Bottner, B., & Emberley, M. (2010). *Miss Brooks loves books (and I don't)*. Alfred A. Knopf.

Brallier, M. (2021). *The doll in the hall and other scary stories: An acorn book* Scholastic[*].

Brown, P. (2014). *My teacher is a monster!: No I am not*. Little Brown and Company.

Buehner, C., & Buehner, M. (2002). *Snowmen at night*. Scholastic[*].

Bunting, E., & Himler, R. (1996). *Train to somewhere*. Scholastic.

Cameron, P. (1961). *"I can't," said the ant*. Scholastic Book Services.

[*]The asterisk indicates this book is included in a series.

Carle, E. (1984). *The very busy spider*. Philomel Books.

Cecil, R. (2012). *Horsefly and honeybee*. Henry Holt.

Cohen, M., & Himler, R. (2006). *First grade takes a test*. Star Bright Books.

Colagiovanni, M., & Reynolds, P. H. (2023). *When things aren't going right, go left*. Orchard Books an imprint of Scholastic.

Cowley, J., & Fuller, E. (2010). *Mrs. Wishy-Washy and the big wash*. Hameray Publishing Group*.

Creech, S. (2003). *Love that dog*. Harper Trophy.

De la Peña, M., & Robinson C. (2016). *Last stop on market street*. Scholastic.

DiCamillo, K., & Van Dusen C. (2005). *Mercy Watson to the rescue*. Candlewick Press*.

DiTerlizzi, A., & Alvarez, L. (2020). *The magical yet*. Disney-Hyperion.

Donaldson, J., & Monks, L. (2018). *The rhyming rabbit*. Macmillan Children's Books.

Donaldson, J., & Scheffler, A. (2006). *The Gruffalo*. Puffin Books.

Draper, S. M., & Watson, J. J. (2011). *The buried bones mystery (Clubhouse Mysteries)*. Aladdin*.

English, K., & Freeman, L. (2009). *Nikki & Deja: Birthday blues*. Clarion Books*.

Fahey, J. C., Shin, S., & Canetti, Y. (2021). *I'll build you a bookcase. Te haré tu propio librero*. Lee & Low Books.

Faruqi, S., & Aly, H. (2020). *Yasmin the superhero*. Scholastic*.

Frazee, M. (2006). *Roller coaster* Voyager Books/Harcourt.

Gibbons, G. (2010). *Alligators and crocodiles* (1st ed.). Holiday House.

Gorman, A., & Long, L. (2021). *Change sings: A children's anthem*. Viking an imprint of Penguin Random House LLC.

Gray Smith, M., & Neidhardt, N. (2020). *When we are kind*. Orca Book.

Gray, K., & Field, J. (2015). *Frog on a log?* Scholastic Press an imprint of Scholastic.

Haley, A. (1974). *Roots: the saga of an American family*. Doubleday & Co.

Hanlon, A. (2012). *Ralph tells a story*. Amazon Children's Publishing.

Heiligman, D., & Bowers, T. (2010). *Cool dog, school dog*. Scholastic.

Ho, M., Meade, H., & Paul, C. H. (1996). *Hush!: A Thai lullaby*. Orchard Books.

Hoberman, M. A., & Emberley, M. (2010). *You read to me, I'll read to you*. Little Brown*.

Hong, L. T. (1993). *Two of everything: A Chinese folktale*. A. Whitman.

Howard, A. (1996). *When I was five* (1st ed.). Harcourt Brace.

Jenkins, S. (2011). *Actual size*. Sandpiper.

Johnson A., & Ransome J. (1990). *Do like Kyla*. Scholastic.

Jules, J., & Smith, K. (2015). *Sofia Martinez: My family adventure*. Picture Window Books a Capstone imprint*.

Jules, J., & Benítez, M. (2010). *Zapato power: Freddie Ramos takes off*. Albert Whitman*.

Kamkwamba, W., & Mealer, B. (2012). *The boy who harnessed the wind: Creating currents of electricity and hope*. Scholastic.

Keats, E. J. (1962). *The snowy day*. Viking Press*.

Keats, E. J. (1967). *Peter's chair*. Viking*.

Keats, E. J. (1990). *John Henry an American legend*. Dragonfly Books A.A. Knopf. Distributed by Random House.

Kerascoët. (2018). *I walk with Vanessa: a story about a simple act of kindness*. Schwartz & Wade Books.

Klassen, J. (2011). *I want my hat back*. Candlewick Press.

Leaf, M., Lawson, R., & Viking Press. (1936). *The story of Ferdinand*. Viking Press.

Leslie, T., & Polk, J. K. (2021). *The story of John Lewis*. Rockridge Press.

Lewis, C. S. (1978). *The Chronicles of Narnia: the lion, the witch and the wardrobe*. Harper Collins*.

Lin, G. (2010). *Ling & Ting: not exactly the same!* Little Brown and Company*.

Lobel, A. (1972). *Frog and Toad together*. HarperCollins*.

London, J., & Remkiewicz, F. (1997). *Froggy gets dressed*. Viking*.

Lyons, K. S., Mallett, K., & Johnson, J. W. (2019). *Sing a song: How "Lift Every Voice and Sing" inspired generations*. Nancy Paulsen Books.

Manushkin, F., & Lyon, T. (2022). *The mystery of the snow puppy*. Picture Window Books a Capstone imprint*.

Markle, S., & McWilliam, H. (2017). *What if you had animal teeth!?* Scholastic*.

Marshall, J. (1980). *George and Martha tons of fun*. Houghton Mifflin Company*.

McElligott, M. (2009). *The lion's share*. Bloomsbury.

McKissack, P., McKissack, F., & Chesworth, M. (2008). *Miami Jackson makes the play*. Random House*.

McQuinn, A., & Beardshaw, R. (2010). *Lola loves stories*. Charlesbridge*.

Messner, K., & Neal, C. S. (2015). *Up in the garden and down in the dirt*. Chronicle Books.

Mitchell, M., & Robertson, M. (2021). *My very favorite book in the whole wide world*. Orchard Books an imprint of Scholastic.

Moore, I. (1991). *Six-dinner Sid*. Simon and Schuster Books for Young Readers.

Mora, P., Parra, J., & Dominguez, A. (2009). *Gracias/thanks*. Lee & Low Books.

Napoli, D. J., & Nelson, K. (2010). *Mama Miti: Wangari Maathai and the trees of Kenya*. Simon & Schuster Books for Young Readers.

Nelson, K., & Rago, M. (2013). *Nelson Mandela*. Katherine Tegen Books.

Neuschwander, C., Woodruff, L., & Burns, M. (1998). *Amanda Bean's amazing dream: A mathematical story*. Scholastic Press.

Olakpe, U., Olakpe, U., & Zermeño, Gaby. (2021). *A is for Agbada: An African alphabet adventure*. Agbada Books.

Orloff, K. K., & Catrow, D. (2004). *I wanna iguana*. Scholastic.

Orloff, K. K., & Catrow, D. (2011). *I wanna new room*. Scholastic.

Pallotta, J., & Bolster, R. (2011). *Who would win? hammerhead vs. bull shark*. Scholastic*.

Paul, C., & Morrison, F. (2009). *Long shot: Never too small to dream big*. Simon & Schuster Books for Young Readers.

Pett, M., & Rubinstein, G. (2011). *The girl who never made mistakes*. Sourcebooks Jabberwocky.

Pilkey, D., & Santat, D. (2014). *Ricky Ricotta's mighty robot (Revised)*. Scholastic*.

Pinkney, J., Grimm, J., & Grimm, W. (2007). *Little red riding hood*. Little Brown.

Polacco, P. (2012). *Thank you, Mr. Falker*. G.P. Putnam's Sons.

Ramsey, C. A., Strauss, G., & Cooper, F. (2013). *Ruth and the green book*. Scholastic.

Reynolds, P. H. (2020). *Say something*. Scholastic.

Reynolds, A., & Brown P. (2014). *Creepy carrots!* Scholastic.

Reynolds, P. H. (2018). *The word collector*. Orchard Books an imprint of Scholastic.

Romito, D., & Freeman, L. (2018). *Pies from nowhere: How Georgia Gilmore sustained the Montgomery bus boycott*. Little Bee Books.

Saltzberg, B. (2010). *Beautiful oops!* Workman Publishing.

Santat, D. (2017). *After the fall: How Humpty Dumpty got back up again*. Roaring Brook Press.

Say, A. (1993). *Grandfather's journey*. Houghton Mifflin.

Sayre, A. P., Sayre J., & Cecil R. (2003). *One is a snail ten is a crab: A counting by feet book*. Candlewick Press.

Selznick, B. (2008). *The Houdini box*. Atheneum Books for Young Readers.

Seuss, S. (1978). *I can read with my eyes shut!* Beginner Books a division of Random House.

Sheffield, H. W. (2020). *Brick by brick*. Nancy Paulsen Books.

Shin, S. Y., Cogan, K., & Paek, M. (2004). *Cooper's lesson*. Children's Book Press.

Sierra, J., & Brown, M. T. (2004). *Wild about books*. Alfred A. Knopf.

Sorell, T., & Frané, L. (2021). *We are still here!: Native American truths everyone should know*. Charlesbridge.

Spires, A. (2017). *The thing Lou couldn't do*. Kids Can Press.

Thompkins-Bigelow, J., & Rose, T. (2022). *Abdul's story*. Salaam Reads/ Simon & Schuster Books for Young Readers.

Thompkins-Bigelow, J., & Uribe, L. (2020). *Your name is a song*. Innovation Press.

Van Steenwyk, E., & Farnsworth, B. (2000). *My name is York*. Cooper Square Publishing.

Verde, S., & Reynolds, P. H. (2020). *I am one: A book of action*. Abrams Books for Young Readers.

Wang, M., Schneider, C., & Runnells, T. (2005). *Who stole the cookie from the cookie jar?* Piggy Toes Press.

Weatherford, C. B., & Nelson, K. (2006). *Moses: When Harriet Tubman led her people to freedom* (1st ed.). Hyperion Books for Children.

White, E. B. (1952). *Charlotte's web*. Harper & Brothers.

White, E.B. (1945). *Stuart little*. Harper & Brothers.

White, E. B. (1970). *The trumpet of the swan*. Harper & Row.

Willems, M. (2010). *Can I play too?: An Elephant and Piggie book*. Hyperion Books for Children*.

Woodson, J., & Blackall, S. (2013). *Pecan pie baby*. Puffin Books an imprint of Penguin Group.

Yolen, J., & Shannon, D. (1992). *Encounter*. Harcourt Brace Jovanovich.

Meet the Authors

 **Krista Calvert**, EdD, is an elementary reading specialist in Kansas City, Kansas, and teaches literacy graduate courses at Avila University. Additionally, Krista collaborates on a blog highlighting multicultural children's literature for a local education nonprofit. Before becoming an elementary reading specialist, Krista worked on literacy professional learning initiatives in urban Kansas City school districts. Krista has taught children from kindergarten through grade 8. She has presented at multiple national and regional conferences on topics ranging from best practices for teaching struggling literacy learners, professional learning frameworks that increase student achievement, meeting kids where they are and who they are in the classroom, teaching with high-quality children's literature, and culturally responsive instruction. Krista advocates for all children to be known as readers, writers, learners, and individuals who matter. You can reach Krista at kristateachingbyheart@gmail.com.

 **Dana McMillan** is an education consultant and has dual degrees in elementary and early childhood education and a master's degree in literacy education. She taught early primary grades for eight years. As an education consultant, Dana has written over 30 teacher resource books and two education curricula, provided consultation to museums, supervised student teachers, and served on multiple design teams, creating interactive experiences for students. She has presented at national and international conferences on topics related to constructivist

theory, including developing learning environments support-ive of children's cognitive, social, and emotional development. Dana spent a school term in a British primary school working in a classroom of 5- to 7-year-olds and later facilitated a group of educators on an educational trip to the same area of England. Dana has a passion for urban education, and much of her work has centered on the long and rewarding process of helping teach-ers become more child-centered in their educational journey. You can reach Dana at danateachingbyheart@gmail.com.

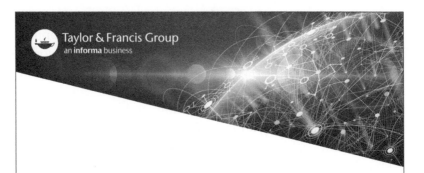

For Product Safety Concerns and Information please contact our EU representative GPSR@taylorandfrancis.com Taylor & Francis Verlag GmbH, Kaufingerstraße 24, 80331 München, Germany